The Scarlet Virgins

Rebecca Lemke

Anatole Publishing, LLC

Printed in the United States of America

First Printing, 2017

Anatole Publishing, LLC
P.O. Box 5611
Norman, OK   73069

Cover and Interior Design by Thomas J. Lemke

ISBN 978-0-9990593-0-2

Library of Congress Control Number: 2017908454

In loving memory of Carol Rae Krueger.

May what she taught me about the love of our Eternal Father shine through.

Table of Contents

The Scarlet Virgins

Chapter 1

Introduction

> *Then one of the elders asked me, "These in white robes - who are they and where did they come from?" I answered, "Sir, you know." And he said, "These are they who have come out of the great tribulation; they have washed their robes and made them white in the blood of the Lamb."*
> *- Revelation 7:13-14 NIV*

You may be wondering about the title of this book, and I have no doubt that you've already formed your own theory about the seemingly contradictory name.

The name is designed to evoke a sense of contradiction commonly found in the minds of people who have grown up in the legalistic Christian movement colloquially known as "Purity Culture." The sense that one, even if technically a virgin, bears a scarlet letter on their soul - a mark that belies a dread that the purity they claim in a physical sense is not enough. It has been compromised, stained by their very existence as a sexual being.

I am writing this book to those who have been wounded by this movement, which places an overemphasis on sexuality, and most especially on the moving target of "purity" that it demands. I personally grew up in an environment where sexuality was simultaneously downplayed (as those in authority sought to minimize its influence on impressionable youngsters), and overhyped (because it was clearly the most important facet of our humanity, such was the rigor with which it was treated and controlled).

You may well have grown up in similar circumstances. You may find yourself feeling soiled for merely entertaining a fleeting thought that you find a member of the opposite sex attractive, convinced that this makes you "damaged goods" for "giving your heart away" (when you have done anything but), and struggling in your walk with God as you wonder how He could love someone so vile. Or you may have abandoned God altogether, fed up with the rules and constraints you feel He has placed on your life that are entirely unreasonable - angry that you were created as a sexual being, but are supposedly prohibited from expressing that fact in any way.

Or any number of other consequences brought about from being raised to believe that your sexuality is, well, dangerous.

In reading this book I want you to come away with but one message: you are not alone, God does love you, and your worth is not found in what you have and haven't done with your body. Moreover, the legalism that has driven you to despair (of one form or another) is not of God, and never has been.

In the coming chapters, we will look together at how Purity Culture came into vogue, beginning against the backdrop of the American sexual revolution - a movement that was anything but pure. From there we will examine the way that many Christians fought back against the rising tide of permissive sexuality, and how this became perverted with legalism that led to its own legacy of the destruction of many young people, both spiritually and physically.

This is all meant to help you to understand how and why these things came to be, as well as where the movement went wrong. This will open the door to healing in your own life by leading us into the truth of the matter: it is not wrong to be a sexual person. In reframing our view of sexuality we can regain a right understanding of who we were created to be, and how we can live as redeemed sinners: ones who have been washed in the Scarlet Blood of the Lamb, and made pure and whole once more.

Chapter 2

Beginning with Clarity

As we begin, I believe it is vitally important to recognize the sensitive nature of the subjects that this book endeavors to cover. The subject of purity is charged with emotion, and that emotion can color our interpretation of what one another is saying. Speaking candidly: this is a very real fear of mine because, during the course of my study and growth on these issues, I have elected to speak out rather than remain silent. In so doing some of my relationships have been strained, and several have been lost, mainly - I feel - due to misunderstandings that were driven by the lack of ability to hear one another properly due to this phenomenon.

Since this book represents the ultimate manifestation of my choice to speak out (particularly as sections of it are heavily autobiographical), and since it will be a one-sided discussion rather than a face-to-face dialogue (as is the nature of books), the need for absolute clarity is multiplied many times over.

With that in mind, in this chapter I will explain my approach and my beliefs regarding this subject, in a way that will (God-willing) place us all on the same page and avoid misunderstanding.

STATEMENT OF PURPOSE

I've been asked this so many times. Why? Why are you

writing this book? Why are you torturing yourself emotionally to get this done? Why is it so important? What is your reason?

So, to start off, I figured I would answer this question.

I am writing this book because of a fundamental belief I hold that every person is made in the image of God (even if they don't believe in Him) and, as such, deserves to know exactly who He really is. Legalism paints us an incorrect picture of God, and this picture is not of a loving, merciful God, but a God that demands beyond human capacity to deliver and is unrelenting in these demands. This puts us in the position of trying to please an impossible deity, recognizing our failure day in and day out, and omits Christ's death and sacrifice so we could be free.

This was the life I lived for close to a decade. Moreover, this is the life some of the people I love continue to live. And for some, this view of God has caused them to reject Him. They recognize that this view is incorrect, but in their pain and suffering, they deem it necessary to walk away from Him in order to find personal healing.

I want to restore the Truth to these people, in its complete and holistic form. The truth of who God is, who they are, and what they are really worth.

Some sections of the book have proven difficult, sometimes due to perfectionism, sometimes due to deep sorrow and trauma, and sometimes due to the simple fact that some things are beyond the vocabulary of this world.

I have chosen to speak out despite these obstacles because I love the people I have written this book for. I believe that through legalism, the character of God is marred in the minds of His children and that is something that I can only describe as evil.

> "Silence in the face of evil is itself evil:
> God will not hold us guiltless. Not to speak is
> to speak. Not to act is to act."
> —Dietrich Bonhoeffer

Statement of Faith

I have noticed in writing and speaking on this subject that people tend to make a lot of assumptions about what I believe or misunderstand me (as discussed above). Our experiences guide what we expect is the stance taken by a person of a certain religious or political background, but sometimes these expectations are completely false. Because of human beings defaulting to this, I want to make sure that my actual beliefs pertaining to the subject of Christianity, Purity Culture, and legalism are made crystal clear at the outset to prevent misunderstandings.

•   I believe in and fully support young men and women who commit to sexual purity.

•   I believe that only God can see what is inside of a person's heart, as we are told in 1 Samuel 16:7 NIV:

> "But the LORD said to Samuel, 'Do not consider his appearance or his height, for I have rejected him. The LORD does not look at the things people look at. People look at the outward appearance, but the LORD looks at the heart.'"

•   I believe that these issues are worthy of discussion and should not be swept under the rug in an effort to conceal dysfunction in the Christian house. As it is so eloquently put in the book *Tactics*, "If we disqualify legitimate discussion, we compromise our ability to know the truth." [Koukl 2009:24]

• I believe a movement that considers itself above reproach is a danger to the Christian church if it claims to be affiliated with it. The New Testament is filled with the Apostles rebuking believers, so why should we, as the modern Christian church, expect to get everything right when history tells us Christians from every era needed correction on one point or another?

• I believe purity is something that God has called us to. It is a gift from Him that we are to guard, but He has not defined it in Scripture the way many people in Purity Culture do.

• I believe it can be very easy to read into the text of Scripture from a modern mindset, but this is one of the fundamental flaws with Purity Culture: a lack of historical context pertaining to the Scripture(s) being used to support it.

• I believe that, while the Bible warns against sexual immorality, there is a distinction between sexual immorality and sexuality and affection. These are not inherently dangerous, as many leaders of the Purity Culture movement have stated, but rather powerful gifts from God.

• I believe that Purity Culture hinges on the question "How far is too far?" At its core, that question is fundamentally flawed and thus everything coming out of the answer is as well.

• I believe, through what I have observed, that Purity Culture utilizes shame and manipulation in order to "get results," and that shame murders intimacy between us and others (especially our spouse), and ultimately between us and God.

• I believe that Purity Culture shifts the way Jesus

wanted us to think about the Law. Our sexual health and purity are gifts that we should be proud to manage with maturity, not a burden that weighs us down and causes us to ask, "Where is the line?" We should be pure because we, as forgiven sinners, want to be, not because we feel that we have to.

• I believe that while we should strive for purity, we should recognize in all of our efforts that God is ultimately the One Who makes us pure.

In sum, my belief is simple: Legalism within Purity Culture is opposed to Christian freedom. Throughout history, the Church has acknowledged the existence of what is termed "Adiaphora" - instances in which a behavior is neither prohibited nor explicitly commanded, and thus is left to the conscience of the individual Christian. By defining sexual sin for our neighbor in a place where the Bible has stayed silent, we are taking the vocation of the Holy Spirit and saying, "Move aside, I can do this better!" This is a dangerous move.

Not only does it challenge God's place as law-giver, but it places the emphasis on our works, and neglects the "Spirit of the Law" in favor of the Letter (and often letters not penned under inspiration, to boot). In addition to that, the sacrifice of Christ is rarely mentioned, if at all, leading many to be beaten down by the Law and left to die, spiritually, without the Gospel.

Not all of what calls itself "Purity Culture" is characterized by legalism

I need to mark the distinction between the purity movement (spurred initially by high teen pregnancy rates) that simply encourages men and women to handle their God-given sexuality responsibly - which is commendable - and the legalistic ugly stepsister known as "Purity Culture." They look very similar because they have much of the same rhetoric, but their messages as a whole are not the same. One does not deviate from Scripture and the other not only deviates, but seeks to add to as well. The catchphrases and words and even thought leaders can be shared. Sometimes even the motivation and the intentions are both good, but anything that threatens to separate us from God needs to be addressed.

Here are some of the legalistic and dangerous aspects of the Christian Purity Culture movement:

1. Teaching that sexuality is dangerous
2. Criminalization of affection, where any affection to one of the opposite sex was equal to having had sexual intercourse, on a spiritual level
3. Works based theology - all or mostly Law, and little to no Gospel
4. Scripture being ripped out of context
5. Rhetoric that ignores forgiveness (e.g. damaged goods)
6. Opinion being passed off as God's word
7. Obsession with sexual sin over and above every other sin
8. Endorsement of lack of sexual education in order to produce results
9. Feelings being treated as evil, untrustworthy, and sinful

Sometimes the legalistic Purity Culture becomes entangled in the healthier movement, masking the danger to many parents. This is a poison that is nearly undetectable because it sneaks in without the knowledge of many, including the teachers.

This is why I have heard so often, "Well, I didn't teach this to my kids. I don't know where they learned it."

Let me submit to you my own experience: My parents didn't raise me with these tenets either, but Purity Culture nearly destroyed my life and my relationship with God. I never attended a "Silver Ring Thing," or a "True Love Waits" conference, nor ever read *I Kissed Dating Goodbye* as a child, and yet the legalism within Purity Culture still managed to reach in and snare my conscience.

Consider this quote from Mark Regnerus' book, *Forbidden Fruit*. He is a researcher on the intersection of religion and sexual practices in America.

> "…Social context matters: What happens around teenagers - including the perspectives and behaviors of parents, siblings, peers and friends - affects their lives, right down to their thoughts, attitudes, intentions and actions." [Regnerus 2007:42]

If this legalism never affected you, I am truly happy for you and I hope it never does, but if you, like me, can see the devastation it has caused in your life or the lives of people around you, then this book is for you.

ADDRESS TO THE PARENTS

This is a note to the parents of the children who have been affected by legalism within Purity Culture.

Parenting is hard. I don't even have a teenager on my hands yet, and I know this. My husband and I already ask ourselves, "What are we going to do when he (our son) becomes interested in girls?"

No doubt, this is a question you asked yourselves too, and Purity Culture presented you with a seemingly good solution!

I want to make one thing abundantly clear: I do not blame you. I know that some of my previous content on my blog and YouTube channel has stirred up controversy, questions, and pain. It has made some people wonder who I was angry at or who I was trying to blame.

This is the truth: I believe parents who teach their children the value of sexual purity are doing a wonderful thing in the eyes of God. Some of the social aspects of the purity movement verge into legalism, which often happens without the parent's knowledge. Most parents I knew who homeschooled did so because they had an overwhelming desire to protect their children from what they saw in the secular culture. While it hurts even me to admit, there is no way to protect your child 100% of the time. Unfortunately, no system is perfect and, in a fallen world, the effects of sin can creep in anywhere.

This doesn't mean you've failed. It means that we live in a fallen world where sin and legalism have corrupted a movement that set out to do good. I believe that parents and children are the victims of its sly tricks and this book is for you, the parents, as much as it is for your children.

Many people might take offense and think I am accusing them of being unreasonable because they followed this incorrect doctrine. I want to clarify that this is not the case. The devil doesn't present us things that are ugly and unappealing to steal us away from God, he offers us things that appear to be good and beneficial. He tempted Eve by saying, eat this and you will be like God! He spins the truth and twists God's gifts. He is skilled, he's had a lot of practice, and we are all vulnerable to his tricks.

Please accept this as my heartfelt, sin-stained attempt at showing you the things that have hurt me and my peers as children. I believe the things I intend to lay out here are important and the cause of much anguish for our spirits. Please take my vulnerability with an open heart and mind. Pray with me, for me, and for all of those affected by this form of legalism.

I want to call out the corruption I have seen within the movement to promote healing and to change the direction for the future. The relationship between you and your child is likely to be strained because of this legalism. Because of fear and shame they might be too scared to tell you.

I encourage you to address this possibility with them. If we never treat a wound, it will fester and infect. And, in the case of a spiritual wound that is left untreated, it can cause spiritual decay and eventually death.

Thank you for having enough interest in your child's spiritual condition to read this book.

ADDRESS TO MY PEERS

I love you. So much.

Life has taken us all on different roads, but our past will always be shared. For myself, it influences every single aspect of my life. Because of you all, I've finally learned to accept it, and your support has strengthened my voice to say all of the things I feel I need to say in light of that. Thank you for supporting me, being there, and listening. It means the world to me. You've helped me to proofread, emotionally supported me while writing some tough chapters, and assured me that this is all worth it.

You've helped me to grow and to learn what it means to be loved by God.

Thank you.

Chapter 3

The Role of the Sexual Revolution

"Do you think society was more immoral in terms of sex during the sexual revolution or now?" I asked my father pointedly, twirling a blade of grass in my fingers as the sun shone down on us in the tiny park near my apartment.

He gave a hearty belly laugh, the kind that only dads can pull off. "Sweetie, there was a woman that walked to Woodstock butt naked. It was in the paper!"

It is one thing to learn facts from a textbook, it is quite another to talk to an eye-witness.

He held my attention as we chased my son around the playground and compared the sexual immorality present in the culture he grew up in with what we currently face.

"They were burning bras! Of course, not many of the guys protested that…" he recounted. "And there were lots of swinger parties. Everyone was having them."

I recall thinking, "They sure didn't teach me this in college…" as he talked about the social climate at the time.

"They were all about doing what felt good and 'free love,'" he said. "Always saying catchphrases like that."

After he was done, I clarified, "So, worse then?"

"Oh yeah," He laughed, "Way worse."

Discussing the sexual revolution in modern society in any way other than positive is often met with disgust and accusations of sexism, misogyny, and holding to Victorian ideals. For Christians like myself, this can make it hard to discuss important implications on society and how the sexual revolution has impacted the Church. While the sexual revolution is a complex historical sequence of events and I cannot possibly fully represent the feelings of any Christian or secularist within this chapter, it is an important conversation to have if we want to understand how contemporary Purity Culture came to be.

As you might imagine, many people in our modern culture view the sexual revolution as a good thing. Others view it as a sign of our country's moral values going down the tubes. I believe that the truth lies somewhere in between, as we will see throughout this chapter.

THE BEGINNINGS OF THE MOVEMENT

Some argue that the invention of penicillin began the sexual revolution in the 1950s because it decreased the rates of syphilis. Others argue that it was the invention of hormonal birth control in the 1960s, which provided a new - and very effective - contraceptive option for the masses. I hold the opinion that both of these inventions touched off the sexual revolution, and for essentially the same reason: they reduce the risk of negative consequences from sexual encounters.

While I believe both of these inventions are morally neutral, holding the possibility to be used for good or evil, there are a wide variety of opinions on these things throughout Christianity. While I would assume that most Christians value the sanctity of life, opinions are varied on whether or not hormonal birth control threatens that. In instances of talking to my Roman Catholic friends, the majority of them are opposed to hormonal birth control, even for health problems, but are in favor of natural family planning. Other segments of Christianity believe there is no risk to hormonal birth control and hold no moral conviction on it. I fall in the middle, believing that some types do threaten life conceived in the womb and others do not. There is a spectrum of opinions on this subject, and discussions on the matter are prone to heated debate.

In the case of penicillin, it is highly useful for treating what before were life-threatening infections. Because this includes certain sexually transmitted infections, some Christians see the invention of penicillin as giving people license to sin by reducing the consequences of sexual encounters outside of wedlock. That is certainly true, but the other side of the coin is that it can also save the life of someone infected through sexual contact in the form of rape.

Already, at the outset of the sexual revolution, you can see that even Christians are divided on whether or not the inventions that started the movement are, wholly or in part, "good" or "bad." There are many other things that came out of the sexual revolution as well, both intended and unintended consequences.

Unintended Consequences

As some Christians were correct in foreseeing, hormonal birth control and penicillin did change the way the sexual market operated. Decreasing the consequences of unmarried sex brought a change in sexual behaviors and patterns.

With the creation of the pill, women were able to control their fertility in a way that was unattainable before. This resulted in loosened attitudes about sex as women could now have sex without (much) risk of pregnancy, making them "equal" with men. The biological ability of men to conduct promiscuous affairs without the risk of nine months of consequences was now something that women were afforded. Instead of trying to rid society of promiscuity, the logic was: "If you can't beat them, join them."

This is unfortunate for a number of reasons. For one, we know as Christians that we should hold ourselves to the standards of God and not the standards of man. This means both men and women should flee from sexual immorality, not towards it. This was exactly what the sexual revolution endorsed though, as one of the many catchphrases that came into vogue was, "If it feels good, do it."

THE BURDEN OF FERTILITY

As a corollary to being able to control their reproductive cycle through the pill, women also gained the ability to delay motherhood for a while, or for forever if they chose to do so. This, along with the Roe v. Wade decision in 1973, which made abortion legal (and anything but safe or rare), gave a false sense of security to those who see fertility as an oppressive burden rather than a wonderful gift. This afforded some the ability to delay marriage and childbearing to be a career woman. Many women since, myself included, have felt pressured to do the same. Young people are encouraged to be stable and successful in their lives and careers before pursuing a family of their own.

While there is nothing morally wrong with having a college degree, a career, a house, and a car before marriage, it does push back the marriage age. This can make leading sexually pure lives more difficult, as some Christian youth have discovered. That is not to say that a young person can't work towards these things before marriage, but staying chaste may require some creativity, sacrifice, and prayer.

Many think of the sexual revolution as an empowering movement, which sounds like a wonderful thing. However, in my own life, I have found this to be false. This is not solely because of my Christian convictions, but equally because of the inconsistency in what the proponents of sexual liberation will support. The empowerment of the sexual revolution is conditional.

FAKE-BAKED EMPOWERMENT

When I was sixteen I was placed on a low dose of hormonal birth control after finding out that I had ovarian cysts rupturing regularly. My OB/GYN was quick to encourage me to "experiment" while I was on it, even offering me condoms to protect against STIs and STDs. To put this in perspective, I had already filled out the extremely aggressive sexual activity questionnaire and had previously informed the doctor that I was a virgin and waiting for my wedding night to have sex. I reiterated to her again my plan to stay a virgin until the wedding, but she insisted I take the condoms. Brandishing my purity ring in defense that I was more than capable of self-control, I asked her if she was really for women's choice or just the choices promoted by popular culture. She rolled her eyes and said that when I came in with a disease or pregnant, she would be saying "I told you so." This was certainly ironic considering that she had praised me in a previous encounter for making the decision to stay pure until my wedding, and bemoaned the fact that most of her patients did not and suffered the consequences.

The OB/GYN's office isn't the only place I have come into contact with this false empowerment. Ironically, for a movement rooted in "empowerment," radical proponents of the sexual revolution like to bemoan what they believe is the unnecessary nature of self-control when it comes to sex. Many only see empowerment as engaging in sexual activities, not the abstinence from sex. This is made clear by the fact that many of them see abstinence as impossible even though, according to their own doctrine, it should be just another sexual choice that is equally empowering as sleeping with someone. They don't just see it as impossible, but as highly offensive because they believe sex is a right in life to which everyone is entitled. Not all of them believe this of course, but in my experience, the majority do.

Despite the fact that they do not value abstinence and other "restrictive" decisions with sex, they do have one thing that they value and see as a moral issue when it comes to sex: consent. They belabor consent as the only moral issue with sex and, oftentimes, only if the perpetrator is a man.

The purpose of sex in the sexual revolution, we are now told, is not about procreation or even love. It is about pleasure: your pleasure. Nothing else matters. Not who you might hurt chasing after sexual satisfaction, not who you infect with a disease you did not disclose because you didn't even know yourself, not your own body which you may render infertile with your escapades. No, the only thing that matters is that you have the most satisfying, exciting sex with whoever or whatever you want (so long as there is consent).

In the book *Forbidden Fruit*, Mark Regnerus makes two telling observations about the current sexual market and landscape. Despite the effects of the sexual revolution, he states, "As a society, we are caught somewhere between understanding it as sacred and thinking it profane." [Regnerus 2007:20]

He also points out that sexual deviance is now a moving target; one that is nearly impossible to pin down given the ever-changing definitions of things like marriage, family, sex, and gender.

This has led many Christian families to say that this generation is the most immoral out of any that has ever lived, though in speaking with my father I am not so sure.

HISTORY REPEATS ITSELF

In my research on this subject, I found that in the early 1850s there arose a trend in England and France predating the American sexual revolution. This movement espoused many of the same values such as drugs, free love, and a focus on sexual pleasure. This was spurred by the Crimean war in the same way America's sexual revolution was spurred by World War II. The ideals matched: nothing is forbidden as long as no one gets hurt. Modesty relaxed, nudity in entertainment was normalized, and pop culture pushed the narrative of "free love." [Luria 1987:14]

For as much as many Christians want to say this is the worst generation in history, there is truly nothing new under the sun. History repeats itself. Society is like a pendulum swinging back and forth from hedonism to legalism. Neither are right, but in our efforts to end up in the middle we usually swing too far and land on one side or the other, at least for a time.

A BRAVE NEW WORLD

We are still being directly influenced by the sexual revolution, even now in 2017. Since the revolution began, we've seen many harmful trends that threaten the stability of the sexual market and the family unit. In the 1970s, cohabitation began to be more common and, despite some radical feminists asserting how empowering their choices are, this choice is one that is shown to harm women. [Kunz 2013:117] No-fault divorce was made legal in all states by 1985, though the primary efforts started way before then. [Kunz 2013:242]

"Open" relationships and polyamory have been esteemed and made popular by shows like Sister Wives. In addition, there are now people working to legalize prostitution in various states. Marriage has been culturally redefined, as has gender, sex, and many other terms relating to sex and sexuality.

People are more concerned with injecting morality into what food they consume than what does or does not happen to their genitals. [Eberstadt 2012:94] Commitment is a thing of the past when pornography, sex robots, sexting, and other forms of sexual immorality are aided by the internet and technology.

One major concern of Christian parents is that of one night stands and hookup culture, which have become more common since the 1980s. [Kunz 2013:83] Hookup culture differs from dating in that sexual encounters often happen on the first date rather than later on and hookups require no commitment or romantic involvement. It can be a way to use another person only for sexual gratification.

This has been made dramatically easier through apps and websites like Tinder and Ashley Madison. These things, like pornography and prostitution, massively change the "cost" of sex on the sexual market. It becomes cheap and easy, and youth who value marriage and purity often find themselves having a difficult time finding a mate who shares the same values. Many women like me find our male peers going for the "cheap" sexual encounters rather than waiting for marriage before becoming sexually active.

LIKE A FROG IN A POT

As you might imagine, all of these things came to be accepted in our society incrementally, and many Christians pointed out that this would happen at the time. They were brushed aside by being told that a little bit of exposure wouldn't hurt, but, of course, we know that is not true. All of these things contributed to the others, leading society further towards leniency and further away from God.

There are a few things that I would consider positive about the sexual revolution, and those are the destigmatization of female sexuality and the emphasis on sex education, including consent and coercion. Unfortunately, these are some of the only positives for those with a traditional Christian worldview. Due to the incremental nature of the consequences of the movement, we are only now beginning to see some of the massive changes in thought that it has brought into our society. Not only has it affected basic definitions, changed traditional ways of thinking about relationships, and glamorized risky sexual behaviors, but there is also a cultic defending of these changes on the part of secularists in order to protect the status quo from "regressing."

During moral conversations with the stereotypical, secular American, you can often find them playing a game similar to slight-of-hand. When you bring up an important topic which is in dispute, the average secular American will substitute an issue of exception to skirt around the logic you are presenting. They will act as though the ideas you hold are contradictory to each other in order to derail the conversation. Oftentimes you may end up defending a topic that you never intended to because they will place you on the defensive and act as though you were defending that strawman/red herring stance the whole time. They may call you ignorant, judgmental, or accuse you of any number of catchphrases and derogatory terminology they keep in their back pocket to rile you.

As an example of this phenomenon, take the subject of abstinence-only education. This is a form of sex ed wherein "the talk" consists simply of scare tactics revolving around STIs/STDs with little to no instruction on anatomy and physiology. This is usually cited by the secularist as a reason that premarital sex should not be off limits when discussing purity. It is posited that, if an individual was fully informed, seeking out sexual experiences as soon as possible would just be a matter of course. Thus, they equate purity with the withholding of information.

What this fails to consider is that teaching the virtue of purity and abstinence-only education are not synonymous. Out of all of the people that I have met who believe that any sexual decision is empowering (as long as it is the one you want), almost none of them have supported abstinence as a reasonable choice. This discussion usually stalemates when neither party is able to convey what they mean. Many people believe that the secularist is more logical and has "won" because they claim that sex is a human right and, therefore, abstinence is abnormal or oppressive.

A SOLUTION?

In this chapter we have seen examples of the rampant immorality stemming from the sexual revolution, and some of the consequences that this wrought on the culture at large. Faced with the inability to discuss traditional sexual norms with the general public, Christian parents were left wondering, "What do we do?"

Many Christian parents recognized that they did have

a significant amount of influence on their children's sexual attitudes, yet they also recognized that the culture around their children informed the decisions those children would make more than anything else. Thus, Christian Purity Culture became the answer to their problem. It allowed many to skirt the responsibility of discussing sex with their child while simultaneously believing that the issue was being addressed through "role models" and purity events.

Christian parents were right to be concerned about the trends they saw, leaving them with no other choice than to remove their children from secular culture.

But did they approach it in the right way? And more to the point, did they go too far?

Chapter 4

Christianity's Response: A Brief History of Purity Culture

The people around me raised their hands and swayed to the music, the acoustics of the youth room carrying the sound to every corner. It was a song I didn't recognize, with movements that were foreign.

Relief settled over me when the melody ended and I no longer had to pretend to know how to mimic the people around me. Visiting other churches was always a challenge for me, especially when it was their youth groups.

I didn't know their rituals. I didn't understand their order of service. And sometimes, I really didn't understand their priorities.

The youth pastor stood at a thin metal podium and began to speak, "Purity is more than sex..."

He launched into a talk about emotional and mental sexual temptation, and I followed along with relative ease. But then he began asking us what dirty words we knew.

This seemed like an odd exercise to me. He wrote them on the board, asking the youth to spell them out instead of saying them. The knowledge of these words, he explained to us, made our minds impure. I thought this was strangely ironic, considering he was practically teaching us every one in existence through this exercise.

He went on to say that what we watched, read, and listened to made us impure. Words were not minced in this conversation. Most of it I agreed wasn't good to watch, but I didn't agree that exposure itself made one impure. Of course, I didn't argue at the time.

The pastor then singled out several popular country bands, stating that we shouldn't listen to them based on the lyrics in a handful of songs. Ironically enough, many Christian parents promoted Elvis (and other older bands) as an alternative, selectively forgetting that he pioneered the racy hip thrusting on stage. The general consensus was that, as long as it was antiquated sexual immorality, it wasn't that bad.

The pastor explained that we could never get our purity back - it was like water that had been spit in or gum that had been chewed. There was also no way to clean our purity - like a barrel of wine with an ounce of sewage dumped in, it was spoiled forever. Hell awaited all who didn't take his message to heart, and with that, we were dismissed.

When I returned home crying that I could no longer listen to my favorite bands and why, my mother was furious.

My mother didn't allow us to go back to that youth event, but the message had already sunk in. Most everything in life could or already had taken my purity, and I needed to do better about avoiding those things or I would face eternal damnation.

CREDIT WHERE CREDIT IS DUE

To be sure, that youth pastor did not invent the concepts he taught us that day, nor did he pioneer the language he used to explain it. With the sexual revolution spreading through the culture like a virus, several Christian thought leaders stepped to the fore, claiming that they had the solution that would protect the youth from succumbing to its siren song.

Parents - afraid for their children, and most of all for their salvation - understandably heeded these authoritative voices. Not all of these voices were wise in their council. Far from it: I believe that the message proclaimed by these men was literally damning in many cases as it drove the children brought up in that context to anger and despair at the false version of God that was taught.

Even so, this book is not meant to focus on these leaders because I believe that it is not in the spirit of love and forgiveness to make this about them. I am not out for blood or revenge; I believe they will answer to God, just as I will, at the end. It is not my place to try to force apologies or enact some sort of payback. The Holy Spirit convicts, not me. With that said, we must examine the teachings of these individuals if we are to understand how Purity Culture fell to legalism.

While I am aware of many such Christian thought leaders - and acknowledge the existence of more people and books that teach similar messages - I am omitting them in the spirit of brevity because they were not a part of my experience with Purity Culture.

Besides this, I believe that nearly all of the literature and thought leaders promote a few overarching and overlapping concepts that are characteristic of the movement. I prefer to direct my attention to these concepts rather than the individuals and books that advanced them.

That is, with one exception, who played an inordinately large role in my own experience, particularly given his young age when entering the fray. I do this because his approach is emblematic of the problems within Purity Culture at large. That person is Joshua Harris, who we will discuss shortly.

A Brief History of Purity Culture

As I mentioned previously, different societies since the fall have swung towards either hedonism or legalism in an effort to strike the proper balance between Law and Gospel, right and wrong, or "freedom and oppression" as the secular culture terms it.

Given the lurch towards hedonism spurred by the sexual revolution in the '50s and '60s, the timing of the counter/corrective movement known as Purity Culture should come as no surprise. A subset of Christian parents swung into legalism in an effort to restore Biblical morality to their community. Also present was the desire to shield their children from the trauma that some of them had endured due to these pleasure-seeking behaviors.

As an aside, the purity movement itself did not begin as an inherently Christian movement. If anything, there is some evidence to suggest that the purity movement began at roughly the same time in both Christian and secular circles, but with slightly different focuses. As evidence of this, *Think Social Problems* by John Carl notes that,

> "Since the mid-1980s, the government has sponsored a number of sex-education programs and most recently has focused on abstinence-only education, which urges youth to wait to have sex and warns them of possible pitfalls of early sexual activity." [Carl 2013:174]

The earliest Christian contribution to Purity Culture began with True Love Waits, an organization that began in the late '80s and early '90s. [Lifeway.com] Similarly, the Silver Ring Thing began in 1995 due to teen pregnancy being on the rise. [Silverringthing.com]

These two organizations consisted of activities like concerts and conferences that promoted abstinence and encouraged the attendees to wear jewelry to symbolize their dedication to "purity" (initially defined as saving sex for marriage). Others saw it as a status symbol or magic token that would protect them from sexual impurity.

Many celebrities bought into the purity movement after going to these concerts and motivational talks, and shortly after could be seen sporting rings, necklaces, and good intentions. The list includes Miley Cyrus, the Jonas Brothers, Selena Gomez, and Demi Lovato, all of which are (or were) major TV personalities on the Disney channel, where they could influence every child allowed to watch their shows (which was admittedly not many homeschoolers, but I digress). In 2001 the number of pledgers was reported to be at or exceeding 2.5 million, even before major public figures had joined the bandwagon. [Regnerus 2007:91]

This all sounds like a very good thing, and that is why so many parents and children bought into it. I begged the question when I wrote for Anne Cohen,

> "…what could possibly go wrong with promoting physical and sexual abstinence when it meant there may be less STIs and STDs, promotion of emotional well-being in regards to relationships, and less teen pregnancy?" [arcwrites.blogspot.com]

This is the mid-swing point on the societal pendulum as it oscillated toward legalism and a redefinition of "purity."

I never attended any of these conferences, but my husband and many of my friends did. While this impacted many people, neither of these branches of the purity movement were the most influential in my life. That title goes to a certain infamous book.

I KISSED DATING GOODBYE

The single most important event to ever affect my relationships with members of the opposite sex occurred when Joshua Harris published *I Kissed Dating Goodbye* in January of 1997.

This book should not have had the impact it did, but many Christians were looking for answers to questions on dating and purity. They gave in to the temptation of hero worship and Harris' words were elevated far beyond what he intended. The Pharisees sought to put extra rules on others for the Sabbath and so too did the Christians of Purity Culture. They wished to make absolutely sure that they didn't get anywhere close to breaking the Law, so they made extra rules to stay as far away from doing so as possible.

What had begun as an emphasis on virginity morphed into what could be done to avoid even getting close to losing one's virginity. Kissing was treated as a gateway drug to sex, and then hugging was treated as a gateway drug to kissing, and so on, until many couples weren't even allowed to have a private discussion before they got married - let alone touch one another. All affection and emotional bonding were deemed dangerous. In his book, Harris asks the reader this:

"For a moment, consider the possibility that even the most innocent form of sexual expression outside of marriage could be dangerous." [Harris 2003:96]

This progression may seem illogical to some, but this was the way many young people within Purity Culture were raised to think. Affection was criminal. Bodies and minds became weapons that could "steal" someone else's purity by merely a thought or anything more intimate than a "holy side hug," as I jokingly call them now. While it is good to be aware and informed of how romantic feelings progress, Purity Culture went above and beyond by utilizing subconscious scare tactics and hyperbolic language in order to keep the youth in check.

As Thomas Umstattd Jr. said in his book, *Courtship In Crisis*, "…someone who struggles with a sin may look down on those who struggle more and create strong rules about that area." [Umstattd Jr. 2015:72]

This, in essence, is how I would describe Harris' book. That is not to say Harris was looking down on anyone, but Harris self-admittedly struggled with sexual temptation. As a result, he created rules in order to combat that struggle. Many parents identified with this same tendency towards lust from sowing their wild oats in their own youth and took his solutions to heart.

In some ways, Harris is a victim of his own good intentions. In his efforts to protect others from the things he endured that were prompted by his sinful nature, he gave a lot of practical advice about avoiding sexual sin. This would have been great if all of his tips were promoted as simply his advice. The problem is that some of it has been promoted as God's word and will for people's love lives instead.

THE LAW OF UNINTENDED CONSEQUENCES

While I disagree with Harris on a lot, mainly due to the

faulty assertions made throughout his book, I don't fault him for the opinions he holds - and I see why many parents picked up the book with such hope. When trying to avoid the sexual revolution and the immorality of the previous generation, people often reacted viscerally instead of carefully thinking through the consequences of the doctrine they adopted.

There were, of course, some outliers. The blogger of *To Love, Honor, And Vacuum*, Sheila Gregoire is one of the only homeschooling parents I know of to have spoken up and advocated for the children in Purity Culture. Her article, "10 Things That Scare Me About 'Purity' Culture," speaks to the problems she foresaw with the legalistic Purity Culture. [Gregoire 2016:online]

Unfortunately, she was in the minority. With an overemphasis on sex from both secular culture and Purity Culture, as well as the twisting of God's word, many children committed to sexual purity out of fear and not out of genuine conviction.

With the proliferation of the incorrect teaching that sexuality is dangerous, you can imagine how this entire situation was a recipe for disaster. Most failed to anticipate the problems Purity Culture would cause and underestimated the social, physical, mental, and spiritual ramifications of the movement. It is to these consequences that we will now turn.

Chapter 5

The Social Consequences of Legalistic Purity Culture

"Have you been raped?" The doctor repeated his question to me.

"What?" I managed to stammer.

"Has anyone touched you?" He rephrased.

"No," I cautiously answered. "Why, what's wrong with me?"

I had been brought in for severe pain in my abdomen, difficulty moving, and trouble breathing - not because I'd been assaulted.

"Are you sure?" He probed in disbelief.

"Yes!" I was nearing hysterics. The nurses had sent my family out of the room for this interrogation.

The doctor sighed, "We're going to have to do a pelvic exam. We don't know what's wrong yet."

"No!" I screamed loudly enough for the entire wing of the hospital to hear.

Startled, the doctor offered up a female nurse to do the exam.

"No." I stared at him in horror, clutching the ends of the thin hospital gown I wore as if it could protect me. Didn't he understand what he was saying?

I demanded my mother be let back in. They hesitantly agreed when I started bawling uncontrollably.

The doctor's questions felt like they had been taken straight out of the sexual assault crime shows my sister and dad liked to watch. The kind where the woman always seemed to be victimized twice, once by the rapist and once by the law enforcement and doctors.

As I tried to recover, the staff spoke with my mother and decided to do some more external testing before resorting to a pelvic exam.

One of the tests revealed that I had a ruptured ovarian cyst and, after some morphine and antibiotics, I was sent home with orders to see a female OB/GYN in town within a few days.

I thought the worst was over until my mother pulled me aside and began explaining in great detail about the procedure known as a pelvic exam, as she believed that the doctor would likely do one. I did not sleep after that. I spent the night before the appointment crying. I considered running away, or physically assaulting the doctor and nurse as a last resort.

In my childhood, I was taught that pelvic exams meant you were no longer a virgin. They were fornication if you were unmarried and adultery if you were. And now I was being told that I would lose something I'd worked so hard to protect over a medical problem I couldn't control.

I considered jumping out of the car on the drive to the doctor because, in my paranoid, sleep deprived state, that seemed like a better option.

Once there I was given a paper thin dress to wear, even worse than the hospital gown, and told to strip. Again they sent my mom away, and again I was probed with intrusive questions and my answers were not believed. As I mentioned before, the doctor commended me on my decision to wait until I was married to have sex, telling me that she wished more of her patients would do the same.

I stared at the dolphin painting on the ceiling, wishing I could be anywhere but the cold medical office with staff that didn't understand the beliefs I had grown up holding. I didn't want to be part of a world in which having plastic forced into your vagina was an acceptable practice. To the doctor's surprise, I breathed a sigh of relief upon learning there would be no exam. l was just glad to have dodged an unnecessary assault on my body.

My mother and I left the office with a prescription for birth control to "keep the cysts under control" and I vowed to never return.

SOCIAL SCRIPTS

Social scripts are the narratives or stories we tell ourselves about our lives and the society we live in. One of the scripts I learned in Purity Culture was that anything that entered the vagina made one impure, including tampons and doctors' instruments. This obviously caused me problems, as it did many other women who grew up in Purity Culture.

This situation, combined with the secular culture at large, offered me and my peers two dueling social scripts.

The main script of Purity Culture told us that sex was bad and that, if we wanted sex, we were also bad (or weak). The main script of secular culture told us that sex was good, there should be no rules, and that partaking as soon as possible was the norm. These two main scripts, or a variation of them, are what many of my peers and I internalized subconsciously.

LACK OF SEX EDUCATION

These concepts drawn from Purity Culture and secular culture were allowed to exist simultaneously in the minds of many, in part because we lacked the appropriate sex education to discern fact from fiction. As we navigated through life and interacted socially with those who were not handicapped by Purity Culture, this lack of important knowledge became obvious in, well, awkward ways.

When I started college at sixteen, I fit in pretty well… most of the time.

Other times, my age and background were evident, and my lack of sexual knowledge a glaring imperfection on my otherwise normal reputation.

One day in business class we were given instructions for a marketing exercise. We received a variety of pictures with which we were supposed to come up with a business that could be marketed from those pictures. The task included giving the business or product a name and a slogan.

A male classmate got a picture of a beach. It was a beautiful image featuring young people in swimwear running into the water. When he stood up to give his business pitch, he was very confident and wore a wide grin.

The professor asked him, "What are you advertising?"

He tried not to laugh as he responded, "Trojan. My slogan is 'wet 'n' wild!'"

The class clapped, except for me.

I naively and fearlessly asked, "What is Trojan?"

My mind had searched through the possibilities that might fit with the slogan, considering things like the Trojan war, a Trojan horse, Trojan computer virus, Trojan my grandmother's accountant…but none of them fit!

The girl next to me laughed and said, "Are you for real?"

"Yeah, I don't know what we are talking about," was all I could reply as my smile fell from my face.

The entire class erupted into a fit of laughter, all eyes on me. After five minutes, the professor finally found the breath to tell everyone to calm down, and then promptly began laughing again. A middle-aged woman took pity and explained the situation to me.

"Oh." I hung my head as I absorbed a newfound knowledge of condom brands.

As soon as class was over, I made my way to my truck in tears as a horde of college boys from the class yelled at me and chased me. It seemed my reputation as a normal college student had been blown to smithereens over an innocent question.

While an intimate knowledge of condom brands is not an integral part of the need-to-know aspects of sex, I have about a hundred and one stories just like this or worse, and many of my peers do as well.

A lack of sex education in general was common in the circles I grew up in. Even when there was the chance to educate us from a Christian worldview in the "purity classes" we attended, the time was wasted on bad analogies about bubble gum rather than the mechanical and physiological aspects of procreation. Again, if there was education in any sense, it focused less on the facts and more on moralization.

The reason we didn't get an adequate sex educations is two-fold. The first reason is that parents generally believed that the more kids know about sex, the more likely they are to act on their sexual urges.

Reason number two is that there was a belief on the part of many parents that their children already knew about sex, or had learned about it from the internet (read: pornography), or their friends.

There are several problems with these two trains of thought. In the first place, the more knowledgeable you are about a certain subject, the better able you are to make a good, informed decision. It's as simple as that.

The second issue is that just because a child learns about sex from a given source doesn't mean they are getting accurate information. You can certainly assume that their peers are not discussing sex the way God intended it to be.

For the record, I don't believe these rationales to be true or helpful. I understand that sex is awkward for parents to discuss with their children, but just because a subject is sensitive does not mean it should be avoided.

There are benefits to an early sex education. For example, as I became educated about sex in my young adult life, I felt more and more confident in my decision to wait until I got married to partake.

I am quite fond of a more holistic approach to sex education, as Mark Regnerus eloquently advocates in his book, *Forbidden Fruit*:

> "In the end, balancing information about sexuality with expectations about boundaries is a rare but optimal approach to a well-rounded, morally sensitive sexual socialization and is appreciated by most teenagers." [Regnerus 2007:204]

What does this kind of approach look like? I think God modeled it through His approach to setting boundaries and teaching Adam and Eve in the Garden of Eden.

Genesis 2:16-17 NIV tells us,

> "And the Lord God commanded the

> man, You are free to eat from any tree in the
> garden; but you must not eat from the tree
> of the knowledge of good and evil, for when
> you eat from it, you will certainly die."

God set clear boundaries with them and informed them of the consequences if they disobeyed His law. They were fully informed of God's command but He did not tempt them - the Bible tells us that God tempts no one (James 1:13).

We (as mankind in Adam), broke God's boundary knowing full well the consequences, and thus strained the relationship between God and man. Still, God gave us choices, and I believe we should do so with our children as well. We should not fear to give them the information necessary to make a fully informed decision.

We can say, "you won't be having sex in my house," and enforce that boundary (and be reasonable in doing so). But at some point, we should trust that we've raised our children in the word of God, and model unconditional love when they make mistakes and are repentant, just as God does with us.

Unfortunately, as I have said, this type of Gospel-centered approach is practically nonexistent within Purity Culture. This leads to a striking dichotomy between this lack of parental involvement in sex education and, in many cases, too much parenting.

Too Much Parenting

The messages of legalism that children hear often include some variation of "my parents don't trust me" and "my parents think I'm bad." As you can imagine, living with the implicit expectation that you are incapable of exercising basic standards of self-control takes its own toll.

My husband likes to tell a story of when he was a teen-ager and his mother would ask him to take out the trash. There were times where he was in the very act of heading towards the trash can, fully intending to complete the chore, when his mother would ask, "Hey, have you taken out the trash yet?" At that point, he would immediately make a bee-line for any other part of the house because, while he was perfectly willing to do as he had been asked, the question coming at the moment of doing so took away his sense of self-determination. In other words, he wanted to show that he could act responsibly without being nagged and the ques-tion stole his opportunity to do that.

What's worse, it actually created an attitude of resent-ment that made him think, "If she doesn't believe I can see to this myself, I'll just let her be right. I won't do it."

This happens within Purity Culture too. We know that sex outside of marriage is not what God intended for us. But the more emphasis our parents placed on it, the more we felt like they expected us to make a poor choice because they constantly repeated the command, often patronizingly, to us.

I know many young adults who will proudly tell you that their first sexual encounter featured leaving their house, go-ing to a friend's house, and having an otherwise unplanned hook-up (while wearing their purity ring for good measure) just to spite their parents after years of too much emphasis on sexual purity. The painful and broken thought process was this: "Fine, if they don't really believe I'm a good kid even when I have worked so hard to be, I'll give them some-thing that matches their narrative of me."

This is often a subconscious decision, one that they sometimes regret, but it shows that the narratives parents impress upon their children are both powerful and important. Oftentimes children will find a loophole in their parents' rules so that they aren't technically breaking them, and one of the loopholes of Purity Culture is called technical virginity.

TECHNICAL VIRGINITY

"Technical virginity" might also be called "anything and everything but penetration," just to get the point across. It is highly debated whether or not technical virginity is on the rise. Much of the research contradicts itself and as such, it is difficult to speak academically on this. The evidence I have is based on personal experience in speaking and interacting with my peers. If you want to know the truth, it is best to find out from the primary sources rather than speculation.

Oftentimes, technical virginity is used to keep the letter of the Law and not the spirit. Many of my friends have engaged in anal sex, oral sex, outercourse, or mutual masturbation before they got married, but rarely sexual intercourse. While the typical American teen performs these activities as foreplay, youth in Purity Culture use these activities, in the absence of penetration, to assuage their guilt at being sexually active. In this way they may remain "technical virgins" while still being able to orgasm and experience sexual pleasure without breaking the Law in the letter of it.

Like many, their consciences are seared from too many extra spiritual rules and no longer operate based on God's word. They have become so exhausted with trying to keep standards higher than God's that they have become spiritually numb. This causes them to seek out things (be it substances, sexual experiences, or otherwise) that will make them feel better about their internalized shame and guilt.

SHAME, OBSESSION, FEAR, AND CONTROL

In addition to the shame within Purity Culture causing issues with healthy sexuality, it can also change body image, cause self-harm, and predispose one to addictions. Eating disorders, compulsions towards cutting or other forms of self-mutilation, alcoholism, drug addiction, and obsessive gambling are just a few things I have observed in connection with growing up in legalism. Correlation does not equal causation, but I do believe that looking more closely at the relationship can tell us something about the "why" behind these self-destructive behaviors.

Legalism is largely about fear and obsession with certain sins. In the instance of Purity Culture, it is the fear of sin and pain combined with an obsession with sex and - to a lesser extent - the physical body. Out of the obsession and fear comes the desire for control.

This is directly contrary to how we should live as Christians. We ask that God's will be done in the Lord's prayer, but often we mean MY will be done. We do not fully trust him to do what is best for us and our children. Just like Eve doubted His command in the garden, we doubt Him now. Is everything really going to be okay? We think that unless things play out the way we want them to, the answer is no. Thank God that in His infinite wisdom, He does what he knows is best and doesn't always let us have our way.

God gave us choices in life, but Purity Culture was (and is) often a way to micro-manage the lives of children, even into adulthood. It placed so much emphasis on virginity and purity that when some children fell short, as the Bible says all people do in one way or another, they did not believe that their parents were safe to talk to. They doubted that they would provide them with unconditional love. Not only that, but because so many of the dictates of Purity Culture were presented as from God, they also didn't believe that God would really love them unconditionally. This is the danger of parents conflating their will and words with God's.

In the absence of having appropriate levels of personal control and boundaries in any area of life, some children will look to other areas to compensate for their inability to make their own choices (and mistakes). Purity Culture is filled with social scripts that encourage crossing healthy boundaries and incorrect attribution of personal responsibility for actions. We will see in the next chapter that this is especially true in the case of sexual assault.

Chapter 6

The Physical Consequences of Legalistic Purity Culture

"I have something I need to tell you," my mother said somberly.

She'd let me sleep in well past 11 a.m., which could only indicate one thing: something was wrong.

There were only two other times I remembered waking up like this, to panicked thoughts of "Why would she let me sleep in this late? Now I'm really going to be behind in math!" Once when a family member got a divorce and once when my grandfather had died suddenly.

My mom had taken all of the phones off of the hook the day my grandpa died, keeping them close so she could answer all of the condolence calls without the ringing waking us up. Today she had done the same, but the phones weren't ringing off the hook like they had that day.

I looked back and noted that her email was open on the computer screen, but I couldn't make out the words.

"What's going on?" I asked her groggily as she motioned for me to sit on her lap. I was ten, and I knew her offering to let a pre-teen sit on her lap meant nothing good was coming out of her mouth. The baby treatment was reserved for serious news.

I elected to sit in my chair at the table and watched as the grave expression on her face morphed painfully when she began to talk.

It soon became clear that there were bigger problems than me being late with my math homework.

Ice filled my bloodstream, her words sending prickles down my back. She smoothed my hair back as I cried, even without fully understanding what had happened.

Rape had always been something fictional to me, something that only happened to strangers and people on TV. Once, my little cousins had been watching an episode of Law and Order SVU on my grandmother's television set, but instead of it being background noise, they were actually paying attention.

"Mommy, what's rape?" one of them inquired, turning to my aunt with wide-eyes.

We all got a small talk that said, in essence, that rape is when a guy hurts a girl. End of story.

The TV got turned off and we never talked about it again, until this day.

My mother, the leader of a quasi-homeschool group in our area, was obliged to explain the horrific situation to me. She told me that in a house we'd been in, someone I saw regularly had taken a sharp kitchen tool, stripped a girl I knew naked, and raped her with the utensil to her neck so she wouldn't scream.

These weren't characters on TV. They weren't strangers. They were siblings. This boy, just five years older than me, was from a "godly" family. I'd been around him regularly for months.

I felt sick to my stomach. I'd always been scared of men because I'd been told that "boys will be boys" and their self-control was lacking due to their visual nature. I had regular night terrors from this fear, and after this happened they became more frequent. My parents would ask me in the morning, "Do you remember what happened last night?" and I'd listen in abject horror as they told me I struggled through the night against someone I thought was raping me.

The uncertainty I felt after these events only increased as the news reached the rest of our community.

SHAME FIRST, ASK QUESTIONS LATER

"I don't think the news is true."

Later on I overheard the adults discussing the rape. At least a few were sure that the police were making the entire thing up.

"She must have done something to provoke him," another parent added.

The general consensus was that if she was raped, it was her fault.

The community response to the rape impacted me more than the original news itself. Hearing the cruel words of people speculating to make themselves comfortable made me wonder whose "side" they would take if I ever found myself the victim of sexual assault. Would it be my fault too?

Their conversation reinforced everything I had ever been told directly in some circles and intuited in others: men do not have self-control, ergo women and their clothing are responsible for sexual assault. Before, modesty was always something expected by our community, but after this what I wore was directed by paranoia. If I saw a man looking at me, I would immediately go into a full blown panic attack and become physically aggressive if approached.

I angrily yelled at many of my male acquaintances for trying to ask me out because, in Purity Culture, asking for a date was the equivalent of asking for my hand in marriage. I felt like this must have meant that I led them on, even though I wasn't interested.

If I acted angry enough and lashed out, I believed they would leave me alone. This was a subconscious decision, of course, but it was nevertheless a powerful one. Despite desperately wanting them to want me, if they acted like they found me attractive I would become inconsolable and physically ill. This led to emotional disassociations when I was touched, even during sports or in passing by male friends. If I didn't disassociate, the pain that overcame me was unbearable.

I couldn't handle the thought of leading them astray, but I desperately wanted to be desired by them. Because of the way emotions and relationships were presented to me in the paradigm of Purity Culture, I thought wanting to be wanted was the same as wanting to be sexually involved, which was not the case for me, but I never put those two things together until much later.

In my mind, the boundaries of who was responsible for sexual sin had always been poorly placed. This was exacerbated by the use of phrases like "guys are visual," "boys will be boys," and "she probably led him on."

These are all things I heard over the years, and many of them were in the wake of this young girl's sexual assault. Some of it was said by people I respected and trusted. I even heard one claim that "he got his five minutes of fun and it was a poor choice, nothing more."

BAD ANALOGIES

This was in addition to the many different bad analogies used in Purity Culture. I remember the ones about chewed gum, spit-in water, and de-petaled flowers. These analogies deemed us irreparably ruined if we committed any kind of sexual sin (which even included: hugging, kissing, having a crush, etc.) before marriage. We were told that everything from music, to innocent affection, to pelvic exams would cause us to be tainted and shatter our purity, making us no longer worthy of someone who had waited.

These all send one clear message: who wants to marry "used goods?"

Unintentionally, this narrative directly opposes the message of forgiveness and salvation found in the Bible by implying that there is no such thing as forgiveness for sexual impurity. In addition, it sent the message that if, God forbid, some depraved individual decided to make a sexual plaything out of you, it didn't matter whether or not you consented, you were now "used" and "dirty." Untold numbers of sexually abused men and women heard that they were spoiled and unworthy, and this message came in loud and clear.

My blood boiled in hearing these things but, as a child, I had no voice. The few times I did speak up, I was silenced with "You'll understand when you are older."

Other people, adults with more authority and life experience than me, told me that this was normal and that it was being blown out of proportion. I spent the next several years fretting over what I wore and how I interacted with men. My paranoia of the opposite sex intensified as I was introduced to the concept of porn.

PORNOGRAPHY

"Please don't tell my parents," he pleaded with me.

I was speechless, nauseous, and had a newfound lack of

respect for the young man who stood in front of me.

He'd divulged to me that during a sleepover with friends he had been exposed to pornography and had "used" it frequently since. At the time, the only knowledge I had of porn was that men looked at it. I did not know that they masturbated to it. Had I known that at the time, I can't even begin to imagine what my reaction would have been.

I felt dirty from this newfound knowledge, just from knowing that I was in the presence of an unmarried man who knew what a naked woman looked like. I'd always been a very private person, refusing to even change clothing in front of female family members. Even at a young age, I had internalized intense shame about my body since my own physical boundaries were repeatedly violated and ignored.

Possessing the knowledge that a young man close to me had crossed such a boundary with a woman, who might not have even consented to have her naked photo on the internet, was abhorrent to me.

This happened to some girls I knew as well; they didn't know where to turn after being exposed to porn, and later developed addictions to it. When you grow up in a culture where sexual sin is the highest offense a person can commit, you don't feel safe turning to anyone for help for fear of being exposed and excommunicated.

After the rape in my community and my initial exposure to pornography as a real threat that influenced the people in my life, I grew even more agitated about my own budding sexuality. I felt that I was a danger to the men around me and, at the same time, that I was in danger of them no matter what I wore. With just a little bit of exposure of my shoulder or a little bit of skin above my knee, I could send one of my friends to hell. Or, alternatively, I could get myself raped.

Despite the fear from these teachings, there was an innate longing present within me to be deeply desired. While I didn't want the power that Purity Culture told me I had over men, I did want to be desired by them in a strong and intensely passionate way.

These two ideas, while at odds with each other, didn't clash in my mind until my wedding night.

Virgin to Vixen

Wanting to be deeply desired and fearing that someone will desire you to the point of assault represent dueling concepts that I and many other women coming out of Purity Culture have struggled with, both before and after marriage. The wedding night causes many women anxiety after years of being told that men are visual, that it was a woman's responsibility to manage their sexuality, and that we are also not supposed to be sexual in any way before marriage.

In saying, "I do," we (as women) are expected to do a 180-degree turn from demure, asexual beings to seasoned, mature, sexually-in-tune women. For those of us with a past in Purity Culture, it seems as though we are supposed to transform from a good girl to the equivalent of a porn star just by speaking our vows.

Throughout my childhood, many of my young friends and I observed quite a few women being blamed for their husbands' affairs. While unmet needs in marriage can be caused by your spouse, you are also responsible for your own decisions and that was a crucial nuance that was never introduced to me as a child.

As a child I was taught that a man's need to cheat was the result of his wife not being desirable enough. This clashed with the fact that we were supposed to be innocent virgins, naive to the way of sexual relations, on our wedding night.

After years of avoiding knowledge about sex, the power of seduction does not magically appear on the wedding night. There is no switch that flips when sex becomes "safe." Many of us, like I mentioned before, were not even given sufficient sex education. We did not know our own anatomy, let alone anything about our husband's, nor the physiology of sex.

In anticipation of this potential problem, I tried to get information to help me just before my wedding. Maddeningly, I only found sources with postmodern ideas that essentially said that anything and everything goes as long as there is consent. These sources encouraged me to go above and beyond what I was comfortable with.

I remember my husband and I standing in the bedroom doorway of our new home together, my wedding dress clinging to me. Despite the fact that it was very heavy and bulky, it felt as thin as paper to protect me from what I knew would happen now that we were home.

The logical emotion was supposed to be happiness, especially after waiting for so long to be able to have sex without shameful remorse or guilt. This was the plan. This was the promise made by many. But, as I stood there, I felt sick beyond anything I'd ever experienced in my entire life.

I felt sick because everyone knew we would be having sex for the first time that night (because my sexual status had been made public with the purity ring I wore). Since we had been public about waiting to have sex, we had given away some of our privacy.

While it is safe to assume that a bride and groom will have sex on their wedding night, for the majority of people in our day and age, the wedding night isn't their first time. For people who do choose to wait, the pressure of the public knowing that they waited can be stressful. Throughout Christian history, it may have been the case that more people were virgins on their wedding day than not, but the emphasis that Purity Culture places on virginity verges on voyeuristic.

I bore an intense emotional burden on my wedding night. The feeling of loneliness while being in the same room with my husband was unbearable. I didn't think he would understand what was going on with me, and truthfully I didn't understand it either.

There was an incredible pressure to perform and to keep my husband and everyone else from seeing that I was falling apart.

But I didn't want to be touched. I didn't want to be looked at. I just wanted to fall asleep.

My husband has always been gentle, understanding, and supportive. I felt like I was the issue because it was my problems that kept us apart. The morning of the following day, I found myself crying in the corner of my bathroom having a panic attack. We always communicated well, yet I couldn't put this storm inside of me into words.

I hadn't been prepared for any of it. I felt violated just from trying to have sex because everyone had always equated virginity and purity. These concepts were directly tied to my worth, and at the point in which I thought I was no longer a virgin, I felt like I would never be whole again. I gave part of myself away within the confines of marriage without knowing the damage it would cause. I no longer cared that I had done the right thing by waiting. What did it matter if I, as a married woman, couldn't have guiltless sex because my body and mind had been destroyed by the dictums of others?

The next few months were filled with a lot of physical,

emotional, and spiritual pain. I had been told for as long as I could remember that sex was dirty. That was a hard mindset to shake, even after marriage.

At the same time, I'd always assumed that sex came naturally, especially since everyone spoke of amazing honeymoons. The more we came together, the more I became numb in order to cope with the depression that had made its home on a bed of shame and anxiety.

While I didn't have a word to describe what happened to me then, I now refer to it as emotional circumcision. This is but one part of a whole complex of mental consequences of Purity Culture.

Chapter 7

The Mental Consequences of Legalistic Purity Culture

"Who do you think wrote it?" one of my peers leaned in to ask our small group of junior-high age girls.

"Who do you think it's for?" and, "Have you gotten to read it?" were among other questions asked in a tizzy of swoons and sighs. It is a wonder that we managed to get to class at our weekly homeschooling co-op that day.

An unsigned love note was the cause of our scattered questions and quickened heartbeats.

We were all beginning to develop crushes, if we hadn't already done so. I had been unfortunate enough to be an early bloomer. A green eyed boy with an ornery smirk had captured my attention by the time I was seven, and I intended to reserve all of my romantic attention for him.

That boy was my childhood crush, and because my community valued courtship over dating, I believed he would be my only crush. Courtship, by the definition I grew up with, meant that the first crush you experienced would be your spouse. Anything less was considered cheating on your future husband or wife. We were told that having a crush was "giving your heart away," a phrase taken from Joshua Harris' *I Kissed Dating Goodbye.*

FORBIDDEN (PUPPY) LOVE

During my childhood, having a crush wasn't considered innocent or acceptable. Having a crush on someone who wasn't your husband before marriage was considered the emotional equivalent of an STD.

This was a stark contrast with how most children outside of Purity Culture grow up. They have crushes, date, are affectionate, and explore their blossoming sexuality without fear.

My mother vaguely knew about my crush, but she rarely teased me about it in my younger years, and almost never brought up my fancy for the boy in question. It was the cause of much embarrassment, sure, but no shame.

Until the love note was passed around.

I remember walking down the hall and wondering if this was what high school would be like; if we could all freely discuss our crushes now. Until this point, we'd kept quiet because we were young. But we were in puberty now, and our bodies and feelings were maturing to prepare us for adulthood.

The excitement of the unsigned note rushed through all of the kids and classes, but a glance towards the table of adults watching us revealed expressions of anxiety and stress. I made a mental note to ask my mother about it when we got home.

As it turned out, she approached me first.

"I know you like him," she started as she sat her purse down on the table. "But I'm afraid you need to keep it a secret."

She went on to explain that the note had caused quite the stir. My mother mentioned that I could get us kicked out of the homeschooling co-op if I let my feelings show and, as a serious child, I took that to heart.

Not long after the note circulated, some women in the group began correcting our bra straps and chastising us for being a temptation to the boys. We were no longer regarded as children or friends; we were dangerous temptresses who would lead our male companions astray.

At this point in time, different forms of segregation between the sexes were put into place because of some teaching derived from Bill Gothard. Talking to a boy without being in a group of people was highly frowned upon. Walking down a hall with a boy without "leaving room for Jesus" (which was never an objective measurement) was a punishable offense.

According to our group leaders, I was a threat to my friends' salvation. My blooming female body was a weapon against men that could be wielded no matter what I was wearing - or so it seemed. I would wear a skirt of the appropriate length, but it still wouldn't be long enough for the nay-sayers. At one point I was prohibited from wearing sandals, presumably because someone's husband had a foot fetish. On paper, I always followed the rules, but it was impossible to adhere to their contrived law.

Not only did our hormones and our bodies change dramatically at this time, but so did the rules we lived by. The teenage years are challenging as it is, and the extra rules made it all the more difficult and confusing. When once we had depended on both our male and female friends for companionship, now we could only rely on people of the same sex. I was taught that my feelings were dangerous and that if I incited feelings in my male friends, I could easily end up physically violated, and would be culpable for the action in question.

To say this another way: I, a naive, young teen who had

just begun puberty, was being taught that the dear male friends I had grown up with and had known for many years were merely a stray bra strap away from losing control of their barely-restrained sexual urges. And if I got caught in the crossfire, I had only myself to blame.

As a child with few to no outside resources to provide balance, I had no reason to assume that anything I was being told was wrong. As a result, I shut down. I buried the feelings I had for the boy, actively and intentionally suppressing them, and panicked every time they resurfaced unexpectedly.

Constantly suppressing my emotions caused a physical reaction. They manifested in misfiring nerves and aching joints - what my counselor would later tell me were the early signs of an autoimmune disease due to stress and unhealthy coping mechanisms. Most of the time though, I couldn't feel a thing, emotionally or physically.

EMOTIONAL CIRCUMCISION, SEXUAL AVERSION DISORDER, AND ASEXUALITY

Christians and secularists alike are in agreement that female circumcision is wrong because it is an abusive, unnecessary, and manipulative way to enforce sexual purity. It destroys the exterior nerves that exist solely for feminine sexual pleasure in an attempt to dissuade the woman from sexual activity. We see this practice as barbaric, but what many fail to realize is that Purity Culture often acts as a sort of emotional circumcision that serves to desensitize, not physical tissues, but healthy feelings and emotions of sexuality in order to achieve the goal of virginity on the wedding night.

As I have talked with people recovering from Purity Culture, a theme has emerged: both women and men often suffered from disassociations when they attempted to have sex. This meant that they felt disconnected from their own bodies and emotions. Some people felt nothing, becoming numb both physically and emotionally as a matter of self-preservation. Because they had been taught that their feelings were shameful and evil in their youth, they rejected their own sexual thoughts and romantic emotions. Honeymoons thus were filled will trauma, not with wedded bliss.

While everyone displays their shame and trauma differently, especially concerning sexual relationships after being raised in Purity Culture, there are a few documented conditions that can occur after growing up in these rigid standards. Sexual Aversion Disorder and "Asexuality" are the ones I have seen the most often.

Asexuality is a term commonly used by those who grew up in Purity Culture and experience a repulsion (or even fear) in response to the idea of sex. It is important to note that this is not the dictionary definition of asexuality (i.e. just a disinterest in sex and a lack of attraction to either sex). What many people who grew up in Purity Culture mean when they use this term is:

Sex and sexuality are disgusting, vile, and repulsive. They make me want to go scrub my skin until it bleeds in an attempt to feel clean, knowing that it will never work, but compulsively doing it anyway.

Sexual Aversion Disorder (SAD) is a bit more nuanced than the "Asexuality" of Purity Culture. With SAD, a person can be interested in intimacy, affection, and romance, but as soon as sexual intercourse is initiated the individual will stop being aroused, even if they want to be. Oftentimes it will become physically impossible to have sexual intercourse due to pain, erectile dysfunction, lack of vaginal lubrication, etc.

Many men and women raised in Purity Culture experience some variation of these things. To them, sex is a violation of their conscience, body, emotions, and more. Some women feel as if they are being raped even when they consent, and some men can experience this as well. There are husbands who describe sexual intercourse with their wives as "rapey" because of the body language their wives give off which indicates the trauma they feel. These women stayed silent because they didn't want to deprive their husbands for fear of driving them to have affairs or use pornography. Quite a few of them tried to ignore their reservations, only to realize they couldn't make them go away.

With these women's lack of ability to connect with and feel their own body, some husbands expressed that they felt as though their wives were emotionally absent during love-making. The wives couldn't reciprocate because they felt paralyzed, and the husbands were helpless to understand what was crippling their new bride. This was not the fairytale ending anyone had in mind.

As most people do these days, some of the folks that I knew turned to the internet for answers. Most popular sexual health resources are a product of the thought process of the sexual revolution and, as a result, can be lacking healthy moral boundaries. Because of this, some of the recommendations Purity Culture survivors find themselves facing include pornography, rape fantasy, and engaging in different levels of BDSM.

RAPE FANTASY, BONDAGE, DOMINATION/DISCIPLINE, SADISM, AND MASOCHISM

When someone has a broken sexuality, they are oftentimes drawn towards deviant sexual behaviors. While it might seem quite the leap to go from a virgin on the wedding night to engaging in such things as a rape fantasy and BDSM, there is a logical, albeit very broken, progression.

The pressure to be a loving wife or a well-performing husband is intense, and the more pressure these people felt, the less they could feel emotionally and physically.

The draw of BDSM and rape fantasy is that it allows the couples, through the lack of responsibility in the encounter, to physically feel, participate, and experience pleasure during sexual intercourse without disassociations or pain. Even if there is a "safe word," even if there is the understanding that it is all pretend, it still gives them a momentary release from responsibility for the encounter, which is ultimately the goal of such things.

If spouse A were to mentally take leave of responsibility for what was happening because they had no control over it, then the feeling of moral culpability for the action in question vanishes. They then become able to freely feel without remorse, guilt or shame. It is only then that they can be present in body and mind and become engaged in the sexual encounter.

These tendencies towards BDSM and rape fantasy in people that have grown up in Purity Culture are quite astounding. I have found that it is quite a large quantity of people, and while I can't point to statistics, I wouldn't say they are anywhere near close to a minority.

There are many other kinds of sexual dysfunction and spiritual degradation that come out of Purity Culture. All of them are destructive and disrupt the gifts and relationships God has given us. As with anything self-destructive in nature, most of it begins with a foundation of self-hatred.

SELF-HATRED

"Bye!" I yelled to my parents as they got into the family van and drove away, my sister accompanying them. I waited until they were completely out of sight before bolting the door and locking it.

They knew I didn't like to travel. I got carsick easily, so they let me stay at home while they ran some errands. I'm sure they thought I was going to watch movies and read while they were gone.

I waited for ten minutes to make sure they wouldn't turn around, in case they forgot something, before pulling out the sharpest pair of scissors I could find.

The blades were cold as I placed them on my developing breast with full intentions of removing it. Puberty had presented a sense of claustrophobia in my own changing body, and continually being told that these changes were harmful to my male companions fueled my compulsion to mutilate my breasts and genitals. It seemed, at the time, the easiest option. I didn't want my male friends to be hurt by my appearance, and hearing that sex was dirty and sinful caused an intense hatred within me of my female anatomy.

I was unsuccessful in this endeavor, by the grace of God, but I harbored the resentment of feeling that the changes my body was going through were simultaneously ugly and dangerous. I was disgusted by myself so much that I hated to look at my developing body in the shower and, on my wedding night, found that I knew little to nothing about my anatomy.

This intense self-hatred that manifested in self-harm compulsions towards "sexual" parts of my body were a direct result of the rhetoric within Purity Culture. Being taught that anything sexual was dirty caused me to internalize feelings that my primary and secondary sex characteristics were inherently dirty. This feeling did not go away with showering, and the compulsion to be rid of those feelings was so strong that I irrationally decided the only way to free myself from them was to remove the body parts that were associated with them.

Thankfully this compulsion subsided for me, but ultimately I and many others developed mental health problems from self-hatred after being told we were never good enough and constantly having physical, spiritual, or emotional flaws pointed out to us. The push to keep up appearances for the sake of "What will the neighbors think" led to secrecy and shame, providing the perfect breeding ground for additional mental health problems and broken intimacy with other people and God.

SELF-HARM

Many folks who grow up in legalism turn to compulsive behaviors and addictions. One of mine was a compulsion surrounding food and my body, and it manifested through anorexia. The modesty standards and Purity Culture I grew up with, which deprived me of self-efficacy when it came to my clothes and actions, led me to seek control over the one thing that I could. That is, my food and my weight. Like most compulsive behaviors, mine was not truly about the weight, and for others, it is not about the substance. Rather, it was about the level of control I had over my own environment and life. The less control I had, the worse it became.

Most of my friends were like me in that they chose their own vices out of an inability to have healthy levels of control over things in their lives. But while my compulsion towards self-harm was largely isolated to puberty, most of my friends and peers continue to deal with the compulsion to inflict self-harm of one kind or another on a regular basis, even to this day.

This comes about because suppressed thoughts and emotions have a psychological impact that eventually can manifest as a physical problem if left unaddressed. Stress, anxiety, and shame have a profound impact on the body. I believe that modern science doesn't even know the half of this yet, though the psychosomatic link is coming under ever-increasing study that is yielding amazing results.

As I mentioned previously, my counselor had several serious discussions with me because he believed that emotional suppression can contribute to the development of autoimmune disorders. Because I was "managing" my anorexia, I wasn't causing any intentional physical harm to myself but, despite this, physical harm was being done. Like me, many other people who have fought their compulsions have the suppressed feelings crop up in other ways like physical ailments from the benign (hives and rashes), to the severe (compromised immune systems).

Your body will eventually find a way to release the psychosomatic tension, whether you want it to or not. Sometimes this suppression makes you numb, where all you want to do is feel something. In the case of cutting - a fairly common manifestation of self-harm in my peer group - your unfelt and unacknowledged feelings can prompt a compulsion to make cuts on your body in order to feel a physical manifestation of the pain you've pushed down. This compulsion can also be due to an internalized belief that you need some form of punishment to cleanse your conscience.

The nights I've spent crying over the fact that people I dearly love have done this to themselves are too numerous to keep track of. If you have hurt yourself, please know that God has seen your sorrow and your pain and He cares. He loves you and he will never forsake you.

ADDICTION AND SHAME

Cutting and anorexia are certainly not the only forms of self-harm that people suffering from Purity-Culture-induced self-hatred end up indulging in. In the absence of the truth and the release that comes through forgiveness in Christ, we seek a release from legalism's obligations instead through addiction. Things like pornography (and sex addiction), drug use, gambling, and alcoholism are all ways in which my peers and acquaintances have dealt with the shame we felt for falling short of legalism's standards.

Because of this shame, legalism tends to isolate individuals from having full and vulnerable fellowship with one another, driving a wedge between them. As I developed my mental health issues in my young life, I felt like I couldn't discuss it with my friends because of the shame. Shame that if I discussed the problems with my male friends, it might inadvertently make them lust after me. Shame that I couldn't be the perfect, strong Christian that they all seemed to be. Shame that I was giving my community a bad name by being broken.

I never reached out for help due to the fear and shame, which in turn made me starved for human affection of any sort. I later learned that my friends felt the same way, but we were all too scared to speak up.

I recently watched a TED talk that really spoke to me. It was about addiction. When we as humans don't have safe people and a community to bond with, we will bond with objects and non-human substances instead. We need bonding to live, and when we can't find it with a human, we will find it with something else. [Hari 2015:online]

We need a community, but not a community that can only heap shame upon us without telling us about the grace and mercy and love and peace of Jesus. Ultimately, our most necessary bond is our bond with God.

Shame kills intimacy, with other people and with God.

PHYSICAL AND SPIRITUAL DEATH

In extreme cases, these compulsive and addictive behaviors my friends and I experienced, coupled with depression, anxiety, and mental health issues, can lead to suicidal ideations and attempts. I have spent many nights trying to talk people in my community down from a ledge. This has happened with varying levels of frequency over time since I was in my mid-teens.

These young people have been hurt, and sometimes, when you are hurt, you lash out at the wrong people, the ones you are supposed to be closest to, because they are "safe." In these instances, many of us lashed out at God and ultimately turned away from Him out of the pain that we experienced.

Many of us wanted to know why He allowed the things He did in our lives, and why He didn't zap our pain away. After feeling ignored, neglected, and angry, many of my peers publicly apostatized from the Christian faith. They confessed that they no longer believed in God and were turning to Agnosticism, Paganism, or Atheism.

Many people believe me to be a good Christian girl, but once upon a time, I did the exact same thing as my peers. I just wasn't nearly as public about it. I told God to take a hike, I didn't need Him anymore. I didn't want to serve someone who would put such a heavy burden on His people, allow them to suffer so much, and leave them to die on a godforsaken planet. I would have rather killed myself at this point than believe God existed and allowed horrible things to happen to myself and the people I loved.

Of course, I did ultimately come back around, as I will talk about in the final chapter of this book. Heart-wrenchingly, there are many others that emerged from legalism along with me who have not.

Chapter 8

The Spiritual Consequences of Legalistic Purity Culture

"Have you heard anything?" I inquired of my hairdresser as she snipped and sliced at my unruly curls.

After a nasty homeschool group split that left my friends scattered, I was beginning my journey to tracking them all down. And, true to homeschooling form, I had no cell phone numbers or email addresses with which to attempt this. While most of my peers had been fairly easy to find, one friend was proving difficult.

"I'm afraid not, sweetie. I'm so sorry," she replied kindly, knowing how much it mattered to me.

Then, after several more months of searching, I found him. Or rather, what was left of him.

He had been uprooted to another country because of a parent's job, but never getting to give him a proper goodbye was the least of my concerns as I gathered new information.

What we had endured in childhood caused massive destruction in his spirit and mind. I learned that in the intervening time between the group split and when I had gotten back into contact, he'd tried to commit suicide multiple times. That alone was enough to cause me to weep and mourn, but unfortunately, that was not all. As a result of the legalism and dysfunctional Christianity we had known as children, he had made the decision to leave the faith.

I knew his suicidal tendencies meant that I might lose him physically, but in an eternal sense, spiritually he was dying as well. The situation was one that I couldn't have ever imagined would happen to any of my friends and, by proxy, to me.

The years took a toll, and he was the first of my friends to blaze a trail outside of mental soundness and spiritual health in the Christian faith. A staggering amount (though any amount is too much) of my childhood friends joined the ranks over time, being driven suicidal by legalism and, ultimately, becoming apostates.

CONTEXT OF SCRIPTURE

Spiritual apostasy doesn't just happen, many factors play into a person leaving the faith. One of those factors is the misrepresentation of Scripture.

While many of the claims of Purity Culture were based on Scripture, leading impressionable children to believe they were all true, I've learned that there is more to Scriptural interpretation than just proof-texting. I now understand that just because someone claims that a Bible verse has a certain application doesn't mean that the application in question is intellectually honest or valid. Scripture is never wrong, but the way in which it is used can be. This is the distinction that many of us miss, and it leads to a lot of confusion.

Scripture is always true, in its proper context. It is the context that helps us get to know the true meaning of the text - what the author intended it to convey.

The verse I heard taken out of context the most was Jeremiah 17:9-10 NIV.

"The heart is deceitful above all things and beyond cure. Who can understand it?"

This verse was used to rationalize the condemnation many girls and boys received for being physically attracted to someone. The misuse of this passage was a routine reminder that the feelings I had, gifts that God had given me to help me navigate the world, were dangerous and should never be trusted. Especially when they were romantic.

But is that what this verse is actually about? Romantic feelings? Or is this just one of many things used to justify putting the children of the purity movement into legalism in order to force us into submission through fear and control?

In this example, Scripture is clearly being ripped from its context, painting a bleak picture that sends one into hopelessness and despair. But, in its context, our eyes are pointed to the Lord, our Redeemer, the one who knows the heart.

This verse in context says,

> "The heart is deceitful above all things and beyond cure. Who can understand it? 'I the Lord search the heart and examine the mind, to reward each person according to their conduct, according to what their deeds deserve.'"

If we look further into the text, we learn that this passage is dealing with the hearts of a nation which has turned away from God, not adolescent puppy love. The situation is one in which God's chosen people were beguiled by pagan influences and turned away from Him, committing themselves to detestable, abominable practices. It is decidedly not dealing with preteens blushing at each other.

Context matters, especially when it comes to the word

of God. One of the biggest problems with legalism is that the people within it aren't knowingly lying. The Scripture they quote is true, but the application they make is not. The Word of God is set in a context of specific situations, and this verse is not set in a situation that can be paralleled with having a crush.

PROSPERITY GOSPEL

In keeping with the theme of misguided information through the incorrect usage of Scripture, variations of a "prosperity gospel" are a common theme in Purity Culture. This is a major issue I have with Joshua Harris' book. He quotes Jeremiah 29:11, a verse that I have heard at every single homeschool graduation I've ever attended. [Harris 2003:86]

> "For I know the plans I have for you," God says, "plans to prosper you and not harm you, plans to give you hope and a future."
> - Jeremiah 29:11 NIV

This verse, along with others like it, are often used to encourage Christians during uncertain times in their lives. The encouragement that people claim it offers is often a lie because many (clergy members included) will use this verse to say that no matter what you are struggling with now, things will get better. In the ultimate sense this is true of course (the Resurrection is the paragon of "better"), but the verse is often applied with a more temporal understanding in place. On that note, I have to say: things don't always get better in this life.

While there is nothing inherently wrong with offering a struggling Christian some encouragement from Scripture, we should strive to make sure our encouragement is Biblically correct and sound.

Let me ask you a question: do you, as a Christian, know what is happening in this passage? Looking at it in context makes it hard to justify the belief that God is telling this to all Christians in all circumstances.

In context, this is a message to the Jewish people who were in exile. The first verse explains:

> "This is the text of the letter that the prophet Jeremiah sent from Jerusalem to the surviving elders among the exiles and to the priests, the prophets and all the other people Nebuchadnezzar had carried into exile from Jerusalem to Babylon."
> - Jeremiah 29:1 NIV

This tells us that the application of the verse as a specific promise to any given Christian is misplaced. As tantalizing as the promise of prosperity somewhere over the horizon surely is, this verse does nothing to give the impression that you, as an individual in your earthly life, will thrive. Actually, it didn't even apply to the Jews as individuals (some of whom would die before they came out of captivity, as verse 10 makes clear). Instead it was meant corporately, since as a group they would flourish even in captivity and return to their land after their sentence was up.

This truth is corroborated by the rest of Scripture and history: the world is full of suffering because it is a fallen world, and all people, including Christians, deal with the consequences of this.

Because of the presence of this prosperity Gospel subtext, many people came away from *I Kissed Dating Goodbye* with the idea that if they followed the formula, they would experience wonderfully passionate and blissful honeymoon sex. This is not the case, and many people are left to deal with mismanaged expectations.

This is in line with a question Mark Regnerus posed in his book, *Forbidden Fruit*:

> "…Are abstinence pledgers and devoutly religious adolescents blowing marital sexuality out of proportion, investing the wedding night with far more significance and anticipation that it can bear?" [Regnerus 2007:96]

This wasn't just a problem that a few teenagers faced, it was a trend that was noticeable Regnerus' research; one which he picked up on in interviews and through statistical data.

Promises were made and expectations set that were impossible to back. Life happens. Sexual dysfunction happens. Medical problems exist. No matter what you do, your life will be tainted by the brokenness of this world.

This is why we put our faith in Christ and the life of the world to come he ushers us into. God has promised that very eternal life to those who believe on His name, not wealth and riches in this life. We need to check ourselves and make sure that our focus is not on earthly gain just for the sake of it.

GOD'S WILL VS. MAN'S OPINION

Prosperity gospel comes about when someone states

their opinion and acts as though it is God's word. This, I believe, is what happened with Joshua Harris' book.

The back cover of his book says, "*I Kissed Dating Goodbye* shows what it means to entrust your love life to God." This is a hefty promise and one that is reiterated throughout the book. The reality is that we have the Bible and the Holy Spirit for this. Scripture tells us what it means to entrust our lives to God. Harris' book shows what his opinions are on the definition of sexual purity and how it can be achieved until marriage. Not marking this distinction is a grave error to make.

While I was writing this chapter, my mother told me, "Oh, I remember that book. People used it as a second Bible back when you girls were young."

And therein lies the problem. The book was written by a fallen man and is not inspired by God, yet people used it as a "second Bible."

This is a common trend in legalism. People like Bill Gothard and Joshua Harris were esteemed and worshiped as idols within many conservative Christian communities. As Christians, we should recognize the difference between God's word and man's opinion, and act appropriately. Everything these men say is based on their own opinion and experiences unless they are directly quoting Scripture in its proper context.

Pet Sins

I've noticed a pattern over the years in the Christian and homeschooling communities, one that also comes out in *I Kissed Dating Goodbye* - particularly in light of Joshua disclosing his struggle with sexual temptations.

The folks I knew who focused on a certain sin, usually

sexual, ended up having major problems with the very sin they were obsessed with. Many men who were outspoken about sexual sins were later revealed to be child molesters, into child porn, or rapists.

A reader left a comment on my blog noting this very phenomenon. She explained to me that her daughter had been a pupil of a Purity Culture leader who had ended up committing adultery. The mother was extremely upset by this and said that the world needed more Christians who "walk the walk, not just talk the talk."

The reason this behavior exists is because of the desire to elevate ourselves over others. We make ourselves feel better by pointing out those who struggle with a given sin more than we do. Consequently, this obsession with pet sins can elevate the sin beyond its proper place and take our focus off of Christ.

ADDING TO THE LAW

Another facet of the problems that come up in legalistic Purity Culture is a tendency to define sexual sin more rigidly than the Bible does.

One can draw an interesting parallel between the thought process of the leadership in Purity Culture and that of the Pharisees in the Second Temple Period of Jewish history. The ones that Jesus verbally sparred with.

In the case of the Pharisees, they recognized that the Jews had previously - by their disobedience to the law - ended up in Babylon as punishment. Their desire was to avoid ever again falling into that kind of captivity. Because of this, they took the law in question, which we know as the Old Testament legal code, very seriously.

The Pharisees fervently sought to keep the law in every

aspect and in all its particulars. But what do you do when a command is not written in exhaustive, no-stone-left-unturned legal language? For instance, how does one "remember the Sabbath day by keeping it holy?" (Exodus 20:8) The text goes on to make it clear that no work is to be done, but what is work? Lighting a fire is one example given (Exodus 35:3), and gathering wood is another (Numbers 15:32). Beyond that, it seems that the Lord was content to allow men a certain degree of freedom, curbed with the injunction against working on that particular day of the week. Flagrant violations were punished, as they should have been, but doing so didn't require parsing out every way the command could be broken.

The Pharisees, however, felt the need to nail things down more completely so as to be absolutely certain that the law was not transgressed upon. As a result, they laid out a complex system to establish every boundary between "work" and "not work" that they could possibly conceive of. This way there could be no gray area, no question about what counted as breaking the law, and no need for the guiding hand of the (sometimes fickle) conscience.

A person who truly desired to follow the spirit of the law would have of course refrained from cooking, farming, traveling great distances, and the like on the Sabbath. However, this type of obedience was not enough for the Pharisees. Their desire to eke out every possible nuance of the command meant that, by the time of Christ, they had even defined exactly the weight above which could not be carried (approximately 1 dried fig), and more besides. [Jewish Virtual Library:online]

Again, their intentions were good. They were trying to create an environment in which 100% obedience was possible without any room for unintentional disobedience. But in so doing, they went beyond what God had said and bound people's consciences with the additional requirements which they imposed. In their attempts to account for every contingency of potential Sabbath breaking, they inadvertently flipped God's order on its head.

As Jesus himself noted in speaking to them, man was not made for the Sabbath, but the Sabbath was made for man (Mark 2:27). What God had created to be a blessed time of rest, received with thanksgiving, became instead an obligation and a burden through the use of these extra commands.

In the same way, those of the Purity Culture movement who issue commands such as "it is unlawful to touch or have feelings before marriage" have a respectable goal in mind. They desire that God's moral and righteous law pertaining to human sexuality and the purity of the marriage bed be upheld. However, as in the case of the Pharisees, these commands have the effect of insisting that man was created for the marriage bed instead of the truth, that the marriage bed was created for man.

WORSHIP OF CREATION

To be certain, elevating that which is created up to a loftier position than it should have is a common theme for mankind.

Romans 1:25 NIV tells us,

> "They exchanged the truth about God for a lie, and worshiped and served created things rather than the Creator - who is forever praised. Amen."

And nothing is more elevated in both secular culture

and Purity Culture than sex.

Secular culture worships much about creation, and this comes as no surprise since secularists reject God and have no reason to worship him over sex or other pleasures of the flesh. Sex is one of the most popular ways that secular culture worships creation. For a modern culture that is constantly changing, this seems to be one thing that you can count on for consistency.

Purity Culture makes this same mistake, but it does so in a different way. It takes the focus off of Christ and places it onto what we can do to be perfect in this life. It makes an idol out of sexual purity.

We desperately need to put sex back into the proper context and return our focus to Christ, our Redeemer.

Lack of Forgiveness

Far from finding redemption in Purity Culture instead of Christ, there seems rather to be a profound lack of forgiveness endemic to the movement. The oft-cited *I Kissed Dating Goodbye* provides us with another good example of this, as Harris starts his book out on the wrong foot and sets the stage for a lot of sorrow for his readers.

He opens with a story based on a friend's dream. There is a wedding in which the bride and groom are standing at the altar. Things get weird when the groom's exes all walk up to the altar and stand with them. This causes the bride to tear up and ask him what gives. He tells her that while these girls don't mean anything to him now, he once gave them each a piece of his heart.

When I read the story for the first time in preparation for this book, I was angry. While I had never laid eyes on it, I had heard it countless times within my homeschooling community. This story, along with Scripture taken out of context, was used to tell us that having a crush on someone was a sinful and unforgivable action that would haunt us in our marriage.

Having a physiological response, like blushing, to someone attractive meant that we had given our heart away to that person. We were told through action and attitude (and some of us, words) that the mere fact that the response existed was the problem. As I noted earlier, any romantic interest in a person outside of the individual we would marry was considered the equivalent of an emotional STD.

After reading Harris' book, I had a few thoughts.

My first thought was that, while I acknowledge that what we do with our emotions and how we train them can be sinful, I do not consider noticing that your genetic material and someone else's might go well together to be morally wrong. God created us to have these sorts of feelings so we could choose a mate and have healthy children.

My second thought was a verse:

> "If you, Lord, kept a record of sins, Lord, who could stand? But with you there is forgiveness, so that we can, with reverence, serve you."
> - Psalm 130:3-4 NIV

Harris' story, in my mind, assumes that we are keeping a record of sins (or in this case, what Harris appears to define as sin). God doesn't do this with us, he offers forgiveness. Yes, if you have fallen into genuine sexual sin, it may follow you into your marriage through STDs and the like. But if God has forgiven you, then you need to also forgive yourself. While there may be a physical ramification for your actions, this does not mean that those actions have not been forgiven.

I question whether how much of his book would have been written had Harris forgiven himself for the things in his past. I also question how much more understanding and gentle the parental advocates of Purity Culture would have been had they done the same.

LACK OF DISCERNMENT

In order to avoid legalism and bad theology, which bears fruit in the manner described above, a certain level of discernment is required of us as Christians. Proper discernment when it comes to theology is vital for keeping the Bride of Christ (The Church) healthy.

For instance: many years before I was born, a pastor that was called to my home congregation had a very short-lived stay. This wasn't due to any sort of medical problem or a new call to a different parish. It was because the man was a heretic. As it stands, he got kicked out by the elders who recognized the errors in what he was saying and took the necessary steps to prevent him from destroying the spiritual lives of our congregants.

In our own lives, churches, and communities, we need to be prepared and knowledgeable so that if we need to give someone the boot, we know why and how to refute and correct the bad doctrine. When bad doctrine goes unchecked, it leads to spiritual abuse, which in turn becomes spiritual degradation and death. I know this all too well from the friends I've lost to apostasy along the way.

SPIRITUAL ABUSE

My experience with spiritual abuse has given me a deep

understanding of the brokenness that is a life touched by lies that claim to be the word of God. Because of this, when spiritual abuse is downplayed among Christians it truly astounds and angers me. We, as Christians, recognize that the word of God is powerful. We confess that with it, God created the entire universe. Even His simple creations, like light, are complex to us.

Many people believe that verbal, emotional, and spiritual abuse are not as important or dire as physical abuse, but consider this: The Bible itself says that the word of God is a two-edged sword that cuts through soul and spirit. (Hebrews 4:12) What becomes of this power in the hands of Satan? He twists and manipulates it in any way he can to turn the Children of God away from their Creator.

This past Sunday, my pastor was talking about Jesus fasting in the wilderness for forty days and forty nights. In his sermon, he pointed out that when Jesus was tempted by the devil, he deemed that the best course of action was to quote Scripture to Satan.

In his life here on earth, Jesus used Scripture to defeat the devil's temptations. If we can recognize that the word of God is extremely powerful, possessing the ability to create and defend against the powers of evil, why is it that when people twist Scripture in spiritual abuse, we as Christians are rather lackluster in our response?

We should not be so afraid of what the world will think of us as Christians that we neglect the spiritually abused among us. Instead of silencing them to save face, we should address their experiences as the severe affront to the Children of God that they are. Spiritual abuse is the most permanent form of abuse. Physical and emotional abuse follow people unto physical death, but if even one person apostatizes from the faith due to spiritual abuse, their fate is an eternal, unending spiritual death.

So I ask you, do you think spiritual abuse, the twisting of God's word - which has the power to create the universe and everything in it and to defend against the devil - is really no big deal?

WHERE DO WE GO FROM HERE?

Spiritual abuse ends in one of a few ways: outright apostasy, agnosticism, codependency with an abusive doctrine, or coming to a right and proper understanding of the faith.

For many, the first three options are their fate, but they don't have to be. If you, like me, believe that God is not who you were taught, then allow me to reintroduce you to our loving Father and what He wants for us.

Chapter 9

Unlearning Legalism

One of the questions I am asked the most is this, "After everything you've been through, why are you still a Christian?"

My answer is simple: I finally recognized that it wasn't God who had hurt me, it was myself and others. Sinful, broken people had projected their own issues and pain onto me. The nature of the God I serve never changed. What did change was my ability to see His nature through how He had already revealed himself.

God is love. We memorized the verse, recited it over and over, but has legalism made us believe something different? After all the rules we heard in the name of God, did you ever question if He really tempts you when the Bible says that He tempts no one? Did you ever feel like He wasn't the merciful God you'd read about in Scripture? Like He could never possibly love or care about someone so dirty? Like you weren't the kind of person He wants in His family because you could never be good enough?

This is the biggest problem with legalism: it doesn't just burden God's children with extra rules, it makes us doubt that He is who He says He is. It makes us question His nature and His unconditional love and forgiveness. It makes us question if He really died for someone so imperfect as us.

The lies we believe about God and what He expects of us can cause us to shrink back from Him. To remedy this, we need to learn the difference between others' opinions and God's expectations. This can be especially difficult for those who have been beaten down by legalism.

After being raised in legalism, things that shouldn't be an issue or cause you any moral or spiritual concern will make you feel the same shame as though you have sinned. There is a bit of practicality in the verse that says "train a child up the way he should go and when he gets old, he will not depart from it." (Proverbs 22:6) It is very hard to unlearn things taught to you in your youth, even if those things are blatantly and obviously wrong.

Legalism destroys consciences. Because you've been taught that things which are permissible are actually wrong, your conscience becomes numb to everything in order to compensate. You simply cannot deal with the guilt brought on by things you shouldn't even feel guilty for in the first place. As a result, your conscience switches off in the name of self-preservation in order to maintain your ability to function when just existing as a sexual being feels immoral. As you might imagine, this comes with side effects.

One of these side effects is that, after a certain period of time, you lose the ability to tell right from wrong. You know the "church answers," but some of those that we were taught are not correct. So how do you distinguish which ones are or are not valid?

As my husband likes to say: in situations like these, it feels as though the ceiling is dark and the lights are shining up from the floor. The shadows on every surface are wrong and opposite, and though your body is telling you that you are right side up, your eyes are telling you that you are upside down. It's disconcerting and even downright horrifying.

In these times, look to Scripture in context. It is Scripture (again, in context!) that is meant to shape our idea of right and wrong. While it might be a learning process, you can unlearn legalism.

Think about all of the times you heard a specific saying or phrase invoking your brand of legalism's pet sin. There are probably a lot, right? Now your job is to read the Bible to see what it actually says, and many times over for good measure. Do this to ingrain the truth into your heart so that you will never doubt. Jesus takes the burden of legalism and the Law so you don't have to.

Aim for that truth, not more lies.

My Plea to You

I want to use this chance to tell you that I love you. Even if I don't know you, even if you hate me, I still love and care about you. Despite my good intentions, I do so imperfectly.

Please allow me to tell you about my Father, whose love is perfect, unconditional, and infinite.

He is not unreasonable, even though the things we were told made Him seem that way.

He is not unmerciful, He is forgiving and gracious.

He understands the struggles you have faced.

He weeps for the hardships that we, His Children, have endured.

Our Lord loves us, and while He maybe hasn't shown this love in the way we've wanted Him too, He has shown it through His Sacrifice of His Son, Jesus Christ.

The Father sent His Son into the flesh, a perfect man, to experience all the perils of this earth. God did this so that He could redeem us through the Son's innocent suffering and death, and so that the Son can say with truth and love: "I understand."

Jesus died for you.

He died for me.

He even died for the people who hurt us.

Why?

Because He is love.

"Whoever does not love does not know God, because God is love." 1 John 4:8 NIV

God's love is more powerful than any force on heaven and earth.

It is greater than our sin. It is stronger than our pain.

It is more infinite than the scars that we bear on our bodies and spirits.

His love is the Truth that shines into the lies and cuts through the deception that has tied us down and trapped us.

God's love sets us free from legalism, our own sinful nature, and from death itself; such is the power of the blood of the Lamb.

> "If I speak in the tongues of men or of angels, but do not have love, I am only a resounding gong or a clanging cymbal. If I have the gift of prophecy and can fathom all mysteries and all knowledge, and if I have a faith that can move mountains, but do not have love, I am nothing. If I give all I possess to the poor and give over my body to hardship that I may boast, but do not have love, I gain nothing.

> "Love is patient, love is kind. It does not envy, it does not boast, it is not proud. It does not dishonor others, it is not self-seeking, it is not easily angered, it keeps no record of wrongs. Love does not delight in evil but re-

joices with the truth. It always protects, always trusts, always hopes, always perseveres.

"Love never fails...

"And now these three remain: faith, hope and love. But the greatest of these is love."
- 1 Corinthians 13:1-8a,13 NIV

When approaching the subjects of sex, legalism, and pain - as I do below - please keep this in mind above all else.

What God Actually Says

Throughout the book, I've mentioned that many of my peers and I were sold an incorrect version of God. What we believed He expected of us was tainted by the opinions of authority figures and was passed off as scriptural truth. Because of this misrepresentation of God, we must, like the Bereans in Acts, search the Scriptures diligently to orient our minds to the truth of His character. In so doing, it helps to ask the right questions.

As with the serpent in the garden, secular culture and Purity Culture ask the same question, "Did God actually say?"

In the case of secular culture, the question is phrased thusly: "Did God really say that you couldn't?"

In the case of Purity Culture, the question is: "Did God really say that you could?"

Both of these are the wrong questions, but they lead us to ask the right one: "What does God say?"

The answer to that question will lead you down a very different path from the ones that secular culture and legalistic Purity Culture had us following. Unlearning legalism doesn't just mean learning who God is, it also means un-learning the lies we've believed about the gifts He has given us.

In this case, the lies surrounding sexuality.

HOW FAR IS TOO FAR?

The question of "how far is too far" that pervades Purity Culture is fundamentally flawed and tends to be where the perversion of Christian freedom begins. The goal in a relationship should not be to go as far as possible; it should be to love and honor the other person.

This doesn't mean you have to marry the first person you date. It also doesn't mean that you won't get your heart broken. But it is entirely possible to grow close to a person without crossing a moral boundary. Affection and attraction felt towards another person are not inherently sinful. These are a manifestation of gifts that God has given you: the ability to choose a mate that is genetically and sexually compatible.

Because of many of the things that we were taught as children, growing close to a person of romantic interest can be anxiety-inducing and spiritually crushing. We are so scared to mess up, "give our heart away," or become impure, but is that really what is happening?

Think of any "friend breakups" you have had for a moment. Do you see yourself as damaged goods now because you gave them intimate details about yourself, talked to them about your struggles, and expected them to be in your future, only to have them exit your life? I would certainly hope not! If that is not the case, do you believe the same about romantic relationships?

I recognize the difference between romantic relationships and friendships, however, there are a lot of false assumptions about romantic relationships in Purity Culture about what "damages" you. With the criminalization of emotional and physical affection, one would think that the physical relationship is the gauge of the spiritual health of the couple. The truth is, you can be affectionate without being sexually immoral, just as you can notice your attraction to someone without it leading to lust. The opposite is also true in that you can lust after someone without touching them at all! Sexual immorality begins in the heart, not in hand-holding or hugging.

That is not to say that you should be physically affectionate just for the sake of being physically affectionate. Song of Solomon 8:4 NIV does say, "Do not arouse or awaken love until it so desires."

My husband and I held off on being physically affectionate until we knew we were getting married, and even then, we proceeded with a plan and copious amounts of self-control.

Everyone is different in how, when, and if God calls them into a relationship, and what works for one couple might not work for another. Some people cannot have long engagements due to sexual temptation, while others can withstand a bit longer of a courtship period.

My best advice is: stay in Scripture instead of asking "How far is too far?" Pray, listen to your conscience, and ask yourself throughout the relationship, "Is this action truly loving to this person, or am I trying to gratify desires of the flesh?" Once you have an answer, act accordingly. If you fall short, seek out private confession and receive forgiveness.

HEALTHY BOUNDARIES ARE A BLESSING

Like most of God's gifts, sex is something that he has given us within boundaries. I cannot count the number of times I've told my son, "You can eat your food without help, but stay in the kitchen!" or "You can go down the stairs without me, but be very careful and pay attention." My motivations are imperfect - I'd rather not clean up a mess or go to the emergency room - but God's motivations for the things He asks of us are not.

Scripture shows us that God utilizes boundaries and treats them as a good and wonderful thing. This is true both in relationships and even in the natural way the world works. When He created the earth, the Bible tells us that He said to the sea, "This far you may come and no farther, here is where your proud waves halt." (Job 38:11)

Boundaries can feel like a bad thing to our sinful flesh, but God in His infinite wisdom has placed them exactly where they need to go when He said we should not commit adultery, fornicate, or give in to any kind of sexual immorality.

Legalistic situations like the ones my peers and I experienced as children can cause the boundary lines of right and wrong to blur. This is a problem, especially for those of us that still value God's word. We want to follow it, but all of the things we have heard and been taught make us doubt what is and isn't true. I still struggle with this in my own life, but I have a bit of advice.

At times when people push their own convictions on you, consult Scripture in context. The Holy Spirit and Scripture can bring you the truth of the situation. Let these things work together to bring you forgiveness and peace in your life. Do not allow legalism to change who you are, because it can and it will. If you give it an inch, it will take a mile and this will continue until you do not even recognize yourself.

Stay in God's word. It will protect you and guide you.

SEX AS A GIFT

When I was young, my parents let me watch a TV show on Disney Channel called "Wizards of Waverly Place." While it wasn't the best use of my time, one episode that really stuck with me. I don't remember all of the specific details of the plot, but what I took away from it was something very akin to the concept of classical conditioning.

One of the characters began to chant, "Chanting makes it important." Soon all of the characters were chanting that phrase in unison, and believing it.

While repeatedly saying something doesn't make it accurate or correct, this is the exact same thing that happened with the culture I grew up in. The unspoken chant that was conveyed through attitudes and actions was something to the effect of "sexuality is dangerous" and "purity is a burden." These things are, as I now know, not true.

God created sex to be a good thing. It is a wonderful act that we can safely participate in within the boundaries He has given us. Purity was never meant to be a burden, and it wasn't meant to be conflated with virginity. Purity isn't achieved by waiting to have sex until you get married because it is not something we can attain on our own. Sex and purity are two gifts from God, and contrary to the impression that many have gotten, they do not contradict one another.

After hearing the chanting that sex is a negative, dirty thing for so many years, you'll need to reverse this classical conditioning with some positive messages about sex.

Surround yourself with people who view sex as a positive and make appropriate distinctions between Scripture and opinion. Look to Scripture for all of the ways in which sex is positive, such as in the Song of Solomon.

Don't be afraid to seek out counseling for this or to find a trusted member of the same sex who is married to talk to about any problems you may be having.

Ultimately, the only one who can heal sexuality that has been broken is the One who created it. I once considered people who prayed about sex a little bonkers, but in recent years I have changed my opinion on this.

When you no longer think of sex as dirty, it no longer seems disgusting to talk to your Creator about it. Pray for the healing of your sexuality, body, mind, and spirit. While we still live on this broken earth we will always face issues, including those pertaining to sex. This is the case whether you waited to have it until marriage or not. But I do believe that God offers healing when we ask, even if it might not be complete in this life.

Throughout this book, I have found myself praying about the past significantly more, and I have found the healing that I sought. It is my earnest hope and prayer that you, through the reading, have found some healing as well.

Managing Expectations

Once you've begun your journey of learning about sex as a gift, you'll also need to assess the cultural norms you've internalized about sex and challenge them if they are unhealthy. Sex isn't everything, but sexuality is a big part of our lives in modern culture. This is why, when it is broken, it spills over into other areas.

Before I got married, I had a lot of misconceptions about sex. I didn't know how the mechanics of it all worked. I was going off of what I saw on TV and what Purity Culture had told me, and neither were correct. Here are some pieces of advice gleaned from my own experience and in talking with other folks like myself.

Both cultures put a lot of pressure on sex, but my advice is to not let these things affect you. Take things slow if you need to and don't feel bad about it. Dump any expectations you've learned from culture or porn like orgasming together, or being completely in sync from the get-go. Drop the idea that women don't enjoy sex or that men aren't romantic. Learn who your spouse is.

Understand that the physical act of having sex is a learning process for many and can take time. You may end up trying a lot of different positions or ways of being affectionate before you find something that is morally, emotionally, and physically comfortable for you and your spouse.

Work through your private thought lives together. Be a safe person for the other to confide in. Understand that lust is a lifelong struggle, not something naturally remedied by marriage. Marriage is an outlet for sexual energy, but it doesn't mean that you won't still have a sinful nature when it comes to temptation and sexual sin. Forgive one another when you fall short. Don't act as though your spouse is perverted simply for wanting something sexually different from what you are comfortable with.

On the other hand, when one of you is in doubt, don't do it! If there is something that one of you isn't comfortable with morally, abstain from that activity. Always go with the conscience of the person who is more sensitive. It may mean "missing out" on some things you want to try, but you won't have the regret later on of violating your partner's conscience.

Don't worry about what you look like. Yes, it is important to stay healthy, but part of being healthy is having a healthy body image. So many men and women struggle with turning their spouse down for sex because they are too self-conscious about their own body. Sex isn't about having a perfect body, it is about spiritually, emotionally, and physically connecting with the person you love.

These things are merely a snippet of the ways in which you can begin to reverse false expectations when it comes to sex. I have found that they are very valuable, both to myself and others.

One more thing to remember is that, as with anything, our motivations can reveal where our values lie. In Purity Culture, this is the difference between focusing on sex or on salvation. This is, in turn, the difference between physical and spiritual life and death. Motivations reveal where we find our identity: in what we do, or in what Christ has done.

What You Are Worth

Sex in Purity Culture has been put forth as something we are defined by. We've been taught that what we have or haven't done sexually is directly tied to our worth. This is the message of both the secular and Purity Culture, even if it wasn't intended.

We were taught from an early age that our virginity was directly tied to our value. It wasn't as if someone came out and said, "You are only worth as much as your virginity," but through the implications of bad analogies and attitudes, many of us got this message. People who weren't virgins were spoken of as worthless, irredeemable, and damaged goods.

Secular culture tells us that our worth is defined by our sexual market value. Sexual market value is, in essence, a measure with which the opposite sex gauges how much they would want to get you in bed. Think of it in terms of the commonly used phrases, "She's a dime piece" or "He's a ten!"

Women throughout the years have been valued on their virginity and sexual attractiveness, while men are valued based on their attractiveness, assets, and sexual experience. Men's worth increases the more they have sex, while women's worth decreases with each sexual encounter.

Everything that the secular culture tells you about your worth is subjective and, as we know, opinions are a dime a dozen. Don't let secular culture define you in anything, especially your worth.

The truth of the matter is that putting our worth in what we have and haven't done sexually is unwise, regardless of which culture tells us to do so.

Our worth should never be tied to whether or not we can resist one sin or another.

When we became Christians, we left behind the standards of measure employed by this world:

> "There is neither Jew nor Gentile, neither slave nor free, nor is there male and female, for you are all one in Christ Jesus."
> - Galatians 3:28 NIV

The Bible tells us in Romans 3:23 NIV: "All have sinned and fall short of the glory of God."

None of us are any better than the other, regardless of an unbroken hymen or "giving our heart away" before getting married.   God doesn't say, "Oh no, this one had sex before marriage, I'm not powerful enough to redeem them." The forgiveness we have in Jesus is more powerful than any past sexual sin.

When God looks at us, He doesn't look at what we have done, He looks at what Christ has done for us.

You want to talk about worth? God loves us so much that He sacrificed His only Son so that we might have eternal life in His name.

This isn't because of any greatness on our part, but because of His greatness. Our focus shouldn't be on what people tell us we are worth, it should be on what God has said about us and done for us.

God's love has saved us, and now it is our turn to love each other.

> "This is how God showed his love among us: He sent his one and only Son into the world that we might live through him. This is love: not that we loved God, but that he loved us and sent his Son as an atoning sacrifice for our sins. Dear friends, since God so loved us, we also ought to love one another. No one has ever seen God; but if we love one another, God lives in us and his love is made complete in us."
> - 1 John 4:9-12 NIV

I beg of you, forgive those who have hurt you, whether they had good intentions or not. Do not let your faith be snuffed out by fear and pain brought on by fellow sinners. Throw off the chains of legalism. Tell one another about the love and forgiveness that Christ gives to us. Live this day and every day forward in God's grace, mercy, and peace. Go forth as a Scarlet Virgin, knowing that your worth is in Him who bought and washed you in the precious blood of the Lamb.

Glossary

Adiaphora

Adiaphora is a concept cited by the early Church and is meant to identify topics that are not expressly commanded nor forbidden by the Law. It describes the areas in life where Christians are given freedom to choose and be led by the Holy Spirit.

Apostasy

When a previously Christian person decides to leave the faith or publicly proclaim they no longer believe in God, this is known as apostasy. Spiritual abuse is a common factor in the decision to apostatize within legalistic circles.

Law and Gospel

Law and Gospel are two Biblical concepts that are often balanced inappropriately within legalism. Ideally, the Law functions by showing us our sins and where we fall short of God's perfect standard. The Gospel shows us our Savior and the good news that we are made right with God in Him.

In Legalism, more of a focus is put on the Law, and very little if any time is spent on the Gospel. This has the effect of spiritually draining and beating a believer down, sometimes to the point of apostasy.

Legalism

A subset of Christian doctrine that deviates from the Bible and includes but isn't limited to the behaviors of: acting as if matters of Adiaphora (Christian freedom) are commanded or prohibited, using Scripture out of context, promoting prosperity gospel, misusing Law and withholding Gospel, and other forms of spiritual abuse and neglect.

PROSPERITY GOSPEL

A false "gospel" in which believers are told that they can expect special privileges in this temporal life on the basis of their obedience to God.

PURITY CULTURE

A culture made up two distinct branches (one secular and one religious) that focuses on the virtue of purity. These branches are set apart by their definition of purity. In the secular branch, purity generally means waiting until marriage to have sex. The religious section can have that meaning, or it can go further to include no-touch courtships and emotional detachment until marriage, which often verges on or crossing into legalism.

The kind of Purity Culture I grew up in is a legalistic movement rooted in the belief that human sexuality is inherently dangerous and must be tightly regulated (controlled) on physical, emotional, and spiritual levels to prevent pain derived from living as a sexual being.

Bibliography

Carl, John D. *Think Social Problems.* Pearson, 2013.

"Encyclopedia Judaica: Weights and Measures." *Jewishvirtuallibrary.com.* May 17, 2017.

Eberstadt, Mary. *Adam and Eve after the Pill: Paradoxes of the Sexual Revolution.* Ignatius Press, 2012.

Gregorie, Sheila. 10 Things That Scare Me About "Purity" Culture. *ToLoveHonorandVacuum.com.* Jan. 19, 2016. Accessed May 15, 2017.

Hari, Johann. (2015, July 9). Everything you think you know about addiction is wrong [Video file]. Retrieved from https://www.youtube.com/watch?v=PY9DcIMGxMs

Harris, Joshua. *I Kissed Dating Goodbye.* Multnomah Books, 1997, 2003.

"History of True Love Waits." *Lifeway.com.* Accessed May 15, 2017.

The Holy Bible, New International Version. Grand Rapids, Michigan: Zondervan House, 2011. Print.

Koukl, Gregory. *Tactics.* Zondervan, 2009.

Kunz, Jennifer. *Think Marriage & Families.* Pearson, 2013.

Lemke, Rebecca. Purity Rings and Good Intentions. *Arcwrites.blogspot.com*. Nov. 30, 2015. Accessed May 28, 2017.

Luria, Zella, et al. *Human Sexuality*. John Wiley & Sons, 1987.

Regnerus, Mark D. *Forbidden Fruit: Sex & Religion in the Lives of American Teenagers*. Oxford University Press, 2007.

Umstattd Jr., Thomas. *Courtship in Crisis: The Case For Traditional Dating*. Stone Castle Publishing, 2015.

"What Is Silver Ring Thing?" *SilverRingThing.com*. Accessed May 15, 2017.

Resources

In leaving legalism, I've had to relearn a lot of the basics of the Christian faith, sexuality, and relationships. These are some of the resources I have found helpful in this journey, and one I have created myself for people like me.

As you consider these resources, please remember to always stretch your discernment muscles, even with trusted sources. I cannot possibly vouch for the theological soundness of every single sentence on a website or book, though I do recommend the following highly.

Boundaries **by Cloud and Townsend** - A must read for anyone who has been abused in any way. It makes the case for boundary setting as a vital practice, and an especially wonderful one for those who are used to being taken advantage of out of guilt and/or shame.

Captivating **by John and Stasi Eldredge** - This book is helpful for women who have conflicting feelings about the nature of femininity.

Courtship in Crisis **by Thomas Umstaddt, Jr.** - This book is healing for those who internalized courtship doctrine and are held captive to a false view of relationship development.

The Good Girls Guide To Great Sex **by Sheila Gregoire** - I recommend this for people who are working through purity culture's messages about sex, as it gives a more holistic view of the subject.

***His Needs, Her Needs* by Willard F. Harley** - This book was groundbreaking for me and my husband on how to understand one another's needs and meet them better. It's a must-have on any newlywed's bookshelf.

***Love & War* by John and Stasi Eldredge** - This book is a great primer on marriage from a holistic and Gospel-driven point of view.

***Quivering Daughters* by Hillary McFarland** - I encourage everyone who grew up in fundamentalism to read this book as it examines the issues with the movement while keeping a balanced Christian perspective, with plenty of autobiography thrown in for good measure.

Song of Solomon - This book of the Bible is helpful for reframing your mindset with regards to the beauty of healthy sexuality.

***To Love, Honor, And Vacuum* by Sheila Gregoire** - This website is helpful for those further along in escaping purity culture.

***Wild at Heart* by John Eldredge** - This is a book for men (and the women in their lives) who want to more fully understand what it means to be masculine from a grace-centered Biblical perspective.

And of course, be sure to check out Scarletvirgins.com for extra content directly related to this book, including podcast episodes and links to interviews with the author!

Acknowledgements

I have a lot of people to thank for helping me make this book a reality.

To my family,

Thank you for putting up with me and my excessive rambling. Without your support and love, this book would not have happened.

P.S. To Mom: I am sorry I called and blew your eardrums out when I tweeted with Joshua Harris and Thomas Umstattd Jr.

Kendall F. Person and The Neighborhood,

Thank you to Kendall, you believed in me when I was just an internet stranger. Your community with The Neighborhood has lifted me up and showed me that the possibilities of what I can achieve are endless.

Drew

Thank you for supporting me through my appearance on your podcast and for being a Beta reader. Your encouragement has been invaluable.

Megan

Thank you for quieting my worries and encouraging me in every step of this process. You kept me going when I wanted to quit.

SHAWNA

Thank you for helping me through writer's block and providing me with a safe space to come when this project became overwhelming. Your encouragement began way before I even wrote the first word, and for that I am grateful.

MY VILLAGE

They say it takes a village to raise a child, and despite the fact that I am no longer a minor, I am still a Child of God. Thank you to my village, which consists of people who have and continue to raise me and point me to Christ.

RACHEL

Thank you for your extensive Beta reader edits, especially the more colorful ones. They no doubt made this book shine brighter than I could have ever done on my own.

THOMAS AND RANAN

A special thanks to my husband and son who put up with my manic midnight writing sprees, reminded me to eat occasionally (or to feed them…), and emotionally supported me through this whole process. My husband not only helped me refine the entire manuscript multiple times (for which he deserves an award), but also did the heavy lifting in creating the cover design and nailing down the final details of the book.

JESUS, OBVS.

It is because of Christ's love and sacrifice that I am inspired to love my neighbor and share the Truth with them.

Author Bio

Oklahoma native Rebecca Lemke grew up in a tiny, conservative homeschooling community. She has learned firsthand that the manner in which we approach modesty and purity can be the difference between life and death, both spiritually and physically. As the result of her deep-seated belief in holistic living, which includes holistic spirituality and sexuality, she strongly advocates for Christ to be our ultimate focus. Rebecca now lives with her husband and toddler, enjoying the simple things in life with them, like root beer and bacon.

Made in the USA
San Bernardino, CA
20 January 2018